STAND AND DELIVER

Written
by
RAMÓN MENÉNDEZ and TOM MUSCA

Adapted for the Stage
by
ROBERT BELLA

Based on a True Story

D1479235

Dramatic Publishing
Woodstock, Illinois • London, England • Melbourne, Australia

STAND AND DELIVER, The Play, premiered February 10, 1995 at the Los Angeles County High School for the Arts. The production was directed by Flora Plumb and included the following:

CAST

Jaime Escalante	Jesse Perez
Raquel Ortega	Sacha Chambers
Tito Guitano	Patrick Martinez
Claudia Camejo	Melanie Guillen
Pancho Garcia	Logan Kincaid
Ana Delgado	Jessica Padilla
Javier Perales	Victor Rodriguez, Jr.
Lupe Escobar	Jaime Doganes
Principal Molina	Leonard Earl Howze
Angel Guerra	Robert Sinclair
Chuco	Joseph Dammann
Rafaela Fuentes	Xochitl Crespo-Oliva
Armando, Maravilla Gang	Julio Colon
Hector Delgado, Student	Daniel Terrazas
Dr. Ramirez, Maravilla Gang	Avelardo Ibarra
Dr. Pearson, Pregnant Girl	Denise White
The Secretary, A.P.Calculus Student	Claudia Coronel
Security Guard, Student	Zachary Aaron
A.P. Calculus Students	Iveliese Arguello
	Dylan Brown
	Melinda Gonzales
	Racheal Perez
Maravilla Gang	Ramsay Davila
	Clea Du Vall,
	Tiffany McGinn
Maravilla Gang, Security Guard	Laura Salwet

PRODUCTION STAFF

Lighting Design . . . . Max Williams
Scene Design. . . . . Flora Plumb
Fight Choreographer. . . . . Penny Jerald
Technical Director . . . . Annette Pillow
Production Manager . . . . Noreen Kimura
Lighting Supervisor . . . . Jonathan Wyman
Voice and Speech . . . . Penny Jerald
Production Stage Manager . . . . Sarah Atkinson
Assistant to the Director . . . . Annie Assatourian
Assistant Stage Manager. . . . . Wendisue Hall
Second Assistant to the Director . . . . Karen Hansen
Assistant Technical Director. . . . . Jo Corbett
Graffiti Artists. . . . . Will Benedict
Pentii Markonnen
Rigoberto Jimenez
Property Master. . . . . Marcus Savino
Costume Coordinators . . . . Jennifer Castro
Chidi Hill
Master Carpenter. . . . . Jaymes Wheeler

STAND AND DELIVER

A Play in Two Acts
For 10 Men, 7 Women
Multiracial/gender flexible (half of the male roles can be
played by females), extras as desired

CHARACTERS

The Faculty:
JAIME ESCALANTE . . . . one of a kind, early 50s
PRINCIPAL MOLINA. . . . tough guy with a heart, 40s-50s
RAQUEL ORTEGA. . . . . a self-assured woman in her 40s

The Students:
JAVIER PERALES . . . . a slim, middle-class boy
TITO GUITANO . . . . . a new-wave math student/musician
CLAUDIA CAMEJO . . . . a moody and sexy fashion plate
FRANCISCO "PANCHO" GARCIA. . . . . a car freak
LUPE ESCOBAR. . . . . an outspoken flirt
ANA DELGADO . . . . a flower ready to bloom
RAFAELA FUENTES a recent immigrant from Guatemala
ANGEL GUERRA . . . . . . a member of the Maravilla Gang

The Community:
CHUCO. . . . . the macho leader of the Maravilla Gang
ARMANDO . . . . the janitor, late 20s
HÉCTOR DELGADO . . . . Ana's father, 45
DR. RAMÍREZ. . . . . a yuppie Latino ETS official, 30s
DR. PEARSON. . . . an African-American ETS official, 30s
and . . .
The Secretary, Security Guards, Police Officer, Various Students
(The Maravilla Gang, Tough Boy, Pregnant Girl, ESL's, etc.)

WRITERS' NOTES

Viewing of the film is recommended and can help to clarify numerous questions.

Double casting of actors in small roles is fine. While the main corps of students is all scripted, a very large part of this play is about the ensemble nature of the unscripted student roles. Escalante's class can be as big as 14 students or as small as the core group of eight. The hallway scenes can and should be fleshed out with specific characterizations and behavior.

There should be an environmental and improvisational approach to the daily life of the school. Set design and staging should also incorporate these aspects. Some suggestions: have the audience pass through security checks, seat the audience in desks, have the students interact with the audience. Certainly there are many more possibilities that can occur within each individual production according to the imagination of the artists involved.

ACT ONE
Junior Year

SETTING: *Garfield High School is represented by a graf-*
fiti-filled classroom and hallway. As the audience files
in, the lights on the stage are dim. It's the night before
the first day of school.

AT RISE: *A police siren wails, closer and closer, flashing*
lights bouncing off the walls of the theater. The sirens
fade out as the lights onstage shift to early morning.
STUDENTS start filing into the space. While there is ex-
citement in the air, it's muffled by the inertia of barrio
life. These are inner-city kids, predominantly Latino;
many are poor. The students range in types, a mixed bag
of jocks, heavy metal aficionados, ROTC's, new-wave
punkettes, **cholos** *(gang members), a few straight ar-*
rows, and ESL (English as a second language) students.
SECURITY GUARDS scan students with metal detectors
as they enter the space. Some STUDENTS are smoking,
some hang out by their lockers or the pay phone, others
cross on their way to classes. Off in a corner, a TOUGH
BOY is selling drugs. In another corner, some GIRLS
are gathered around a PREGNANT GIRL, feeling her
stomach and gossiping. JAVIER PERALES enters the
classroom. The desks are arranged haphazardly. He

slides one toward the front and sits in it. He opens a copy of a science-fiction novel and reads intently. A few STUDENTS enter the classroom. One grabs JAVIER's book and throws it in the trash. JAVIER gets up and retrieves it. OTHER KIDS grab ass, make out and laugh. General mayhem. A Latino Rap beat comes from the boombox of a just entering TITO GUITANO. TITO wears a jeans jacket with the image of Christ painted on the back. He coolly enters the classroom and sits, still lightly bopping his head to the music. Enter JAIME ESCALANTE. There's a slight stoop to his rolling walk but there is nothing weak about him. He is met by one of the SECURITY GUARDS.

SECURITY GUARD. Are you a teacher?

ESCALANTE. Yes, I am. I'm new.

SECURITY GUARD. Gotta see an ID. *(Bewildered, ESCALANTE gets his driver's license out and gives it to the GUARD. The GUARD refers to a clipboard.)* You're not on my list. *(Into radio.)* Uh, Main Office, got a guy here says he's a teacher... "Jaymee" Escalante...

ESCALANTE *(leans toward the walkie-talkie, saying his name with the correct Hispanic pronunciation). Jaime* Escalante. I am here to teach computer science.

SECURITY GUARD. No computers here. *(Chuckling.)* Sure you're at the right school?

(Enter RAQUEL ORTEGA with a Los Angeles POLICE OFFICER. Abrupt and charming at the same time, she is used to dealing with problems in a no-nonsense way.)

POLICE OFFICER. Anything else missing?

ORTEGA. Just the key to the ladies' room. *(ORTEGA spots ESCALANTE and comes to his rescue.)* Mr. Escalante, glad you made it! Raquel Ortega, chairwoman of the math department. *(To SECURITY GUARD.)* He's on the faculty.

POLICE OFFICER. And where exactly was the fecal material found?

ORTEGA. In my office. You'll know when you're near it. *(The POLICE OFFICER makes a note. ORTEGA starts leading ESCALANTE off.)*

ESCALANTE. The computers? They weren't stolen, were they?

ORTEGA. I'm sorry, Mr. Escalante. We were supposed to get computers last year and the year before and there's no funding again for them this year. Let me show you to your classroom.

ESCALANTE. But, you don't understand. I was supposed to teach computers.

ORTEGA. Welcome to Garfield, Mr. Escalante. *(They exit. A bell rings. The behavior of the kids in the classroom grows more chaotic with the sounding of the bell. CLAUDIA CAMEJO crosses near TITO's desk.)*

TITO. So, where were you last night?

CLAUDIA. What do you mean, where was I?

TITO. I was *waiting*.

CLAUDIA. Oh, you were waiting, huh?

TITO. Yeah, and I was dreaming about you.

CLAUDIA. Good. Keep dreaming. *(CLAUDIA gives him a playful slap and wanders off.)*

(Enter ESCALANTE. His entrance has absolutely no effect on the kids. If anything, they become more rowdy.

PANCHO GARCIA slides over to ESCALANTE and imitates every gesture the teacher makes.)

PANCHO. You our new teacher, man? Hey, you the teacher?

ESCALANTE. Will everyone please try to find a seat? ...

PANCHO. Hey, what are we gonna do today?

ESCALANTE. Please take a seat.

PANCHO. Sure, no problem, "Teacher Man." *(The STUDENTS heckle ESCALANTE's efforts.)*

ESCALANTE. For those of you who cannot find a seat, please stand against the wall. *(There are about 25 students and only 15 desks. TITO grabs a passing CLAUDIA and sits her on his lap.)*

TITO. Hey, let's put our desks in a circle and discuss our feelings, huh?

ESCALANTE *(overlapping).* Okay, all right. One body to a desk.

CLAUDIA. Could we talk about sex?

ESCALANTE. If we talk about sex, I have to give sex for homework. *(The STUDENTS react with catcalls, laughs, and whistling. CLAUDIA gets off TITO's lap.)*

CLAUDIA. You know, I could get you fired for saying that.

ESCALANTE *(overlapping).* Stand back everyone, please... Move back.

ESL STUDENT #1. **Que dijo?**

ESL STUDENT #2. **No sé.**

ESCALANTE *(to ESL STUDENTS).* **Entienden inglés?**

PANCHO. Sometimes... *(Some STUDENTS laugh. ANA DELGADO tries to defend the ESLs.)*

ANA. Come on, you guys... *(More laughter.)*

ESCALANTE. **Los que no entienden inglés, por favor le-vanten la mano.** *(More hooting from the STUDENTS and most raise their hands in a pretense of ignorance.)* Please move forward if you do not speak English. **Los que no hablan inglés, por favor, pasen al frente.** Please, for all the first row, please stand up.

ANA *(relinquishes her seat, turns to JAVIER)*. Javier.

JAVIER. No. *(JAVIER, in his front row seat, does not move. Several ESL STUDENTS move forward and sit in the front row.)*

ESCALANTE *(to JAVIER)*. What's the problem?

JAVIER. I was the first one here.

ESCALANTE. I'll find you another seat, okay, Johnny?

JAVIER. My name's not Johnny. *(ESCALANTE erases graffiti in order to write his name on the board.)*

ESCALANTE. Okay, okay, I make a mistake. No problem. My name is Mr. Escalante and I teach... *(Refers to course description.)* Arithmetic 1-A. *(JAVIER stubbornly reads from his book. ESCALANTE closes JAVIER's book and points to the back of the class. JAVIER reluctantly gives up his seat. Jeers and whistles from the other STU-DENTS. ESCALANTE picks up a textbook and writes on the blackboard: 31 lbs. – 19 oz = ? (While writing.)* Okay. Chapter 1. Weights and measures. Start simple: 31 pounds minus 19 ounces equals what?

TOUGH BOY. Pounds of what?

ESCALANTE. Whatever you want.

TOUGH BOY. I have 31 pounds of dope and sold 19 ounces.

TITO. If you had 31 pounds you'd be pretty stupid to be here in school. *(The CLASS breaks into laughter.)*

ESCALANTE *(to CLAUDIA)*. Do you have the answer?

CLAUDIA. I don't have to buy drugs, he gives them to me. *(More catcalls and laughter.)*

ESCALANTE. If he gave her 19 ounces, how much would he have left? Anybody? *(JAVIER raises his hand. ESCALANTE nods to him.)*

JAVIER. Twenty-nine pounds, 13 ounces. *(Some STUDENTS smack their lips and hiss "Lambe" to JAVIER. He shoots them dirty looks.)*

ESCALANTE. That's right. Way to go, Johnny. *(ESCALANTE writes on the board: 1,872 ÷ by 23. While writing:)* You keep that up and you'll go back to head of the class. Invent the hyper-drive for a spaceship. Computers. Science fiction, science fact. Okay. 1,872 inches divided by 23 inches. *(STUDENTS snicker. Someone burps loudly. ESCALANTE turns to the class, no hands are raised.)* Who's got the answer? C'mon, this is easy. Anyone can do. You, in the plaid shirt.

PLAID SHIRT *(mischievously)*. 1,895.

ESCALANTE. Why did you add them? How many of you don't know what this means? *(ESCALANTE points to the long division sign.)*

PANCHO. I don't need no math. I got a solar calculator with my dozen doughnuts.

LUPE. The bus is exact change, no big deal. *(Laughter from the class.)*

ESCALANTE. Okay, okay. Quiet! *(The bell rings. The STUDENTS rush out of the classroom, cheering and laughing. They nearly trample a confused ESCALANTE. He checks his watch, then hears a voice offstage. ESCALANTE crosses out into the hallway.)*

MOLINA *(offstage)*. Everyone back in their classroom!

(PRINCIPAL MOLINA enters the hall. The STUDENTS groan and start to clamor as he ushers them back into the classroom.)

MOLINA. Back! Back in class! That was a premature bell!

PANCHO. Premature bell? I thought we weren't supposed to discuss sex in class.

MOLINA. All right, sit down. Sit down! Stop talking! *(MOLINA goes to the window and looks out through binoculars.)*

ESCALANTE *(joins MOLINA)*. Principal Molina.

MOLINA. Mr. Escalante, please, call me Hugo.

ESCALANTE. Is it a fire drill?

MOLINA. No. Sneaky little bastards rigged the bell. *(The bell rings again and STUDENTS break for the doors screaming and laughing. MOLINA races after them shouting. The halls fill up as if the day was just beginning. MOLINA continues from offstage.)* Class is not over yet! Get back inside!

(Alone in the classroom, ESCALANTE surveys the damage. The walls are filthy and covered in graffiti. He shakes his head and slowly starts to pick up the trash the STUDENTS left on the floor. The lights fade up into a tableau of the school. A spot comes up on PANCHO. As PANCHO speaks, we see ESCALANTE straightening up the desks and cleaning up the classroom in the background.)

PANCHO. Let me tell you something about school. Besides the fact that it sucks—you got all these dense teachers tryin' to brainwash you into thinkin' the way they do. I mean, like I really want to think like them. "Those who can, do. Those that can't, *teach*." That's what Uncle Nando says. He dropped out of school when he was younger than me. Talked himself into a job as a carpenter's apprentice. Now, Uncle Nando's like 32, and runs his own construction company. I mean, he's got it *made*. He don't even gotta work Saturdays if he don't wanna. Got a big-screen TV right in his office. Drives a bitchin' Trans Am that's already paid off. I'm tellin' you, the chicks are all over his shit. As soon as I get a decent job, I'm outta here. Probably start as an apprentice mechanic. This way I can get parts for my car at a discount. I got a '74 Mustang, and as soon as I start bringing in the dough, I'm gonna fix the body, paint it candy-apple red, turn the rims inside out, install a stereo system you can hear a block away and get my engine purring like a tiger. *Roaaaow*!! Shit, by the time I'm Nando's age, I'll be the boss of my own body shop. *(Like an exaggerated TV commercial.)* "You got a problem with your car take it down to Pancho's. Ten percent off to any woman who wears a dress up to here." *(Laughs at his own joke.)* Hey, I know some of you are thinkin', this **carnal** up here is full of himself. But I really know how to get around. I'm a walking road map. Ask anybody in Garfield. I get anyone anywhere fastest way possible, guaranteed. *(Rapid fire.)* El Dorado Disco in Long Beach? Even though it seems out of the way, jump on the 5 to the 710. Unless it's rush hour. Then you take Soto to Slauson, left on Atlantic but skip the light and cut through the Thrifty's parking lot, then you're on Atlantic all the way out to Ocean, make a right and then you hit Shoreline. And you can put pedal to the metal on the way home 'cause the cops don't use radar at night. See? That's why I'm in no hurry. 'Cause I know where I'm going. Won't be long 'fore I'm cruising around in the fiercest piece of machinery in East Los. Pick up any **ruca** I want. That's right, man. Shit. Don't need no high school diploma for that. *(Lights fade out.)*

SCENE TWO

AT RISE: *The first day of school is long over. The STU-DENTS have left and so has most of the faculty. ESCA-LANTE has spread out newspapers on the floor of his classroom. He's surrounded by painting supplies. MRS. ORTEGA stops by and peeks into the classroom.*

ORTEGA. Mr. Escalante, is everything okay? The security guard told me you were staying late.

ESCALANTE. Needs some paint. Then it will only smell bad.

ORTEGA *(smiling)*. Be careful. If the school board sees the faculty making repairs, pretty soon they'll have us sweeping the hallways.

ESCALANTE *(smiling back)*. It'll be Top Secret.

ORTEGA. Bear with us, Mr. Escalante. Students can sense a new teacher's frustration. I'd hate for them to take advantage of you.

ESCALANTE. Mrs. Ortega, I'm not a new teacher. I taught for years at a Jesuit school in Bolivia.

ORTEGA. Yes, of course. But Garfield students are a bit different than Jesuit students. You can see for yourself, it's a tough school.

ESCALANTE. I like tough schools. It's no good unless the kids work hard.

ORTEGA. By "tough" I mean...Mr. Escalante, one of our "kids" tried to stab another kid in the schoolyard today with a compass he stole from geometry class...A lot of them only show up because they get a free lunch...By next year, half your class will be dropouts. **Desaparecidos.**

ESCALANTE *(gently).* Mrs. Ortega, if these kids are in school I can teach them more than adding and subtracting. You have me teaching basic arithmetic five periods in a row. I taught *physics* to barefooted Indians in the Altiplano.

ORTEGA. If we can teach them to count their change, balance their checkbook, maybe learn a trade, then we've educated them. With these kids it's not like—are they going to college, it's more like—are they going to make it home? *(Beat.)* Mr. Escalante, I hope coming back to teach wasn't a rash decision on your part. Every year we get well-intentioned people going through a mid-life crisis. They want to do something meaningful with their lives, then quit on us after two weeks...

ESCALANTE *(looking at the walls).* Might need two coats.

ORTEGA. Mr. Escalante, next time you want to do something outside your job description, please, check with me first. Good night. *(ORTEGA exits. ESCALANTE looks at the painting supplies, a bit disappointed. He sighs, then starts to prepare the walls to be painted. The lights slowly fade out.)*

SCENE THREE

AT RISE: *The bell rings and the lights come up on the classroom. The newly painted walls are in stark contrast to the graffiti in the hallway. STUDENTS are filtering into the room. ESCALANTE is at the head of the class looking over a seating chart. The STUDENTS pay little attention to their teacher.*

ESCALANTE. ... Garcia, Guitano, Perales, and Santos. All right, these are your permanent seats for the rest of human history. Any problems with this, too bad. *(The STUDENTS begin to settle into their newly arranged seats, but the chatter continues nonetheless.)* 2x plus x plus 1. Who's got the answer?

PANCHO. We're supposed to add the alphabet? *(Snickers and chattering.)*

ESCALANTE. Too hard for you **burros?** Okay. How about 9 squared?

TITO. The only square around here is you, man. *(Laughter and more talking.)*

ESCALANTE. All right, all right ... You like to talk, that's okay ... Let's talk *numbers.* C'mon, you like to talk. Give me some numbers! C'mon! *(Some STUDENTS continue to talk, some throw out numbers, being as disruptive as they can. PANCHO is reading a car magazine. TOUGH BOY stands an his desk and screams.)*

TOUGH BOY. 738!

ESCALANTE. More!

PREGNANT GIRL. 365. *(ESCALANTE lists the numbers on the board as they are called out, some in English, some in Spanish. Part of the class begins to get caught up in the game and the room fills with shouted numbers and laughter.)*

ESCALANTE *(overlapping)*. More! More!

STUDENTS. 433. 327. 634! 248! 751!

ESCALANTE. Okay! Okay! Okay! Stop! *(The class briefly settles down. ESCALANTE prowls around the room looking for a victim. He spots PANCHO reading his magazine.)* Hey, Motorhead! You bring your calculator today? *(Some STUDENTS laugh and repeat the nickname. PANCHO pulls out a solar calculator. ESCALANTE walks back to the board.)* Okay. I'll make you a deal. You add these numbers faster than me and you can read your magazine. I win, I get the magazine *and* the calculator. *(STUDENTS giggle and ad-lib, "Yeah right," "Go ahead," "Go for it, Pancho," "Motorhead." PANCHO smiles, contemplating his victory.)* It's a deal? All right. Go! *(PANCHO quickly enters the list of numbers into his calculator. ESCALANTE adds the numbers on the board, writing the answer, but starting with the numbers in the left hand column instead of the right. Students egg PANCHO on, but ESCALANTE finishes long before him: 3,496.)* Motorhead, you done yet? What'd you get? 3,496! Is it right? Is it right?

PANCHO *(looks up from his calculator, annoyed)*. Okay, yes! It's right!

ESCALANTE *(patting PANCHO's belly)*. Stay away from those doughnuts, they slow you down. *(Some STUDENTS groan, some cheer and laugh as ESCALANTE takes PANCHO's magazine and calculator.)*

VARIOUS STUDENTS *(overlapping)*. You cheated! You did it backwards. No way! How'd you do that?

ESCALANTE. I can tell you the secret!! But you guys don't like math. You like Mickey Mouse classes. You want me to tell you? Okay! Math is simple. Anyone can do!

LUPE *(to CLAUDIA)*. This guy's loco. *(A paper airplane whizzes by ESCALANTE's head. STUDENTS are still giggling and heckling.)*

ESCALANTE. You see! You don't like math! You like airplanes! But you know what an airplane is? It's *math*. It is! Aerodynamics. Relation to forces! *G-loads!* What else you like? *(STUDENTS shout out things, laughing and teasing each other. "Cars," "Basketball," "Drugs," "Cellular phones," "Girls," "Roller-coasters." ESCALANTE prowls the room, like a cross between a cheerleader and a bulldog; always in motion, cajoling, mischievously feigning punches, teasing. ESCALANTE continues, overlapping.)* Cellular phones! For cellular phones you need to know about math! They cost so much! Okay, c'mon! Give me an example of something where you don't need math.

PANCHO. Race car driver.

ESCALANTE. Power-to-weight ratio... Race cars use *downforce*, upside down aerodynamics, to get more grip from the tires. More grip—more speed—better handling. Talk to the girls, they know. Better handling, you win the race!

CLAUDIA. You got that right. *(Some STUDENTS make catcalls.)*

ESCALANTE. Engineering, astrophysics. Anything you do, you're going to need math. It's the language of the future! They're gonna outlaw words. Only gonna use numbers! Name something else!

TITO. Rock star! *(The kids laugh and cheer.)*

ESCALANTE. Math is the foundation of music. Tempo!
  Quarter notes, eighth notes, half notes. Beethoven was
  my first student! Try again, Johnny. *(The STUDENTS
  begin drumming on desks to "Oye como va," or making
  any kind of musical noise they can think of. ESCA-
  LANTE dances to his desk. He opens his briefcase and
  puts on a chef's hat.)* All right, all right, quiet. Quiet!
  I'm a bad man. Could hurt you good. *(With some cere-
  mony, he pulls a meat cleaver from the briefcase, and
  thwacks it down into his wooden desk. STUDENTS
  snicker and heckle.)* Okay. I warned you. This is serious
  business. *(ESCALANTE puts on an apron, With the
  cleaver he goes at several apples like a sushi chef. Some
  giggles and ad-libs.)*

PANCHO. Look like Julia Child. *(Finished, ESCALANTE
  cleans the blade with a small towel and places the
  cleaver on his desk. He moves about the room distribut-
  ing pieces of apple. ESCALANTE walks with a sense of
  purpose, never smiling or breaking the mood. He ends
  up near CLAUDIA and quickly asks her:)*

ESCALANTE. What you got?

CLAUDIA. It's an apple. *(Everyone laughs.)*

ESCALANTE. *How much?*

CLAUDIA. What do you mean? *(A few STUDENTS giggle.
  ESCALANTE moves quickly to LUPE.)*

ESCALANTE. What you got?

LUPE. Half.

ESCALANTE. Goot. Excuse me my German accent. *(More
  giggling. ESCALANTE approaches ANA DELGADO at
  the back of the class.)* What you got? *(ANA draws into
  herself as her teacher gets closer.)* What you got?

ANA *(whispering).* Missing 25 percent.

ESCALANTE. What? I got wax in my ears.

ANA. Missing 25 percent.

ESCALANTE. That's right. Missing 25 percent. Is it true intelligent people make better lovers? *(This breaks the KIDS up. ESCALANTE turns quickly to PANCHO. PANCHO is devouring his apple.)* Hey, what you got?

PANCHO *(the core in his mouth).* I got a core. *(More laughter.)*

ESCALANTE *(overlapping).* You owe me a hundred percent. And I'll see you in People's Court. Everyone, please open your book, Chapter 2, page 26. Multiplication of fractions and percentages.

(The class is interrupted by the entrance of ANGEL GUERRA and CHUCO. CHUCO's got a hard look, baggy pants, white shirt buttoned at the collar, long black coat and sneakers. ANGEL wears a t-shirt and a net on his head. The room gets quiet.)

ESCALANTE *(pointing to apples).* Twenty-five percent, 50 percent, 75 percent, and a hundred percent. *(CHUCO and ANGEL approach ESCALANTE with the casual swagger of gang kids.)*

CHUCO. Who's calling the shots, ése?

ESCALANTE. Got a slip? *(CHUCO holds out his slip to ESCALANTE. Before the teacher can take it, CHUCO lets it fall to the floor. ESCALANTE picks it up. To ANGEL.)* You got a slip? *(ANGEL just sniffs and looks at the ceiling. The class silently observes the confrontation.)* Okay, you'll have to stand in the back until I get another desk. *(To CHUCO.)* You sit right here, okay?

(ESCALANTE makes JAVIER give up a front row seat. JAVIER grimaces, but doesn't fight. He stands and joins a few other STUDENTS standing against the wall. Over JAVIER's cross.) Everyone please read the first paragraph. *(Softly to CHUCO.)* Where's your equipment?

CHUCO. What you mean?

ESCALANTE. Paper?

CHUCO. Don't got any.

ESCALANTE. Pencil?

CHUCO. Don't got any.

ESCALANTE. Got to come to this class prepared.

CHUCO. Do the work in my head.

ESCALANTE. Ohhhh. You know the times table?

CHUCO. I know the ones, the twos, and the threes... *(On "threes," CHUCO flips ESCALANTE the finger. A few GANG MEMBERS laugh, egging CHUCO on.)*

ESCALANTE. Finger Man. I heard about you. Are you the Finger Man? I'm the Finger Man, too. Do you know what I can do? I know how to multiply by nine! Nine times three. What you got? *(ESCALANTE holds up 10 fingers, with his palms toward CHUCO. Then, with his left hand he counts off three fingers. The third one he bends in half. He wiggles the two fingers on one side of the bent middle finger, and the seven fingers on the other side during the part of the answer that corresponds to the number of fingers held up.)* Twenty-seven. Six times nine. *(Counting fingers.)* One, two, three, four, five, six. What you got? Fifty-four. You wanna hard one? How about eight times nine? One, two, three, four, five, six, seven, eight, what you got? Seventy-two. *(The bell rings. ANGEL and the rest of the STUDENTS begin to file out. To CHUCO.)* Stay put. I want to talk to you, man. *(To class.)* Please make sure you do problems one through 20. Page 26.

PANCHO. Can I have my magazine, Mr. Escalante?

ESCALANTE. Don't bring it to class again, all right? *(As PANCHO exits, ANGEL deliberately bumps him. The MARAVILLA GANG, CHUCO's army, has followed ANGEL back into the room. ESCALANTE notices that he is alone with the GANG, cut off from the exits.)*

CHUCO. **Sabe qué, ése?** Don't get excited. *(CHUCO walks past ESCALANTE to the desk and picks up the meat cleaver. He fingers it during his lines, smiling.)* Y'know, cut me a "D" like the other profes. I'll read my funny books, y'know, count the holes in the ceiling. Kick back.

ESCALANTE. First thing I can teach you is some manners. *(ANGEL steps forward and mischievously reaches for a pencil in ESCALANTE's pocket.)* I wouldn't do that if I was you. Might lose a finger. Won't be able to count to 10.

CHUCO. We've seen **vatos** like you before. *(CHUCO slams the cleaver down into the desk. ESCALANTE flinches. CHUCO smiles easily.)* You'll be hurting soon.

ANGEL *(tap-slaps ESCALANTE on the cheek)*. **Ponte trucha,** huh? *(Exit ANGEL, CHUCO, and the GANG. ESCALANTE removes the cleaver from the desk and returns it to his briefcase.)*

(Lights shift. ANGEL appears downstage in a pool of light. He is smoking. Upstage, ESCALANTE begins to hang posters of famous sports figures on the walls of the classroom. ANGEL watches him, then faces the audience. ANGEL snaps his fingers and causes the lights to fade down on ESCALANTE. ANGEL smiles at his power.)

ANGEL. Now you in my classroom. Ain't teachin' no pinche math, y'know. Not here, homes. Not in East Los... *(ANGEL looks around the room.)* Ever see somebody die? *Bam! Bam! Bam!* And the **carnal's** dirt nappin'? I don't think so. Man, sometimes a **vato** gets killed, he don't die. Not right away. Had to steer my bike through three different gang territories just to make it to sixth grade. I was still a **mocoso** when I started out a baby tagger. My homey did buses, but I could climb... reach the heavens, spray paintin' the signs over the freeway. It was a joke, a game that turned to war. *(He assumes a gang pose.)* You've seen the stare. You return the stare, you challenge me... Your fear is my friend. Night my homey got permanently taxed, we were down by the street corner. Having a good time, brown-baggin' some brew, forgettin' our cares... A car drives up slow... Shots ring out—one, three, two loose **balas**. My homey shot in **el pecho** and shoulder. My **carnal,** who had never let me down was next to me **sufriendo** and all I had was a **pinche** bruised elbow... I held him tight and tighter... Tryin' to keep him **vivo,** y'know, puttin' up a big "stay away" sign, flashin' "no trespassing," so **la muerte** would not take him away... Took three hours to die. Three hours. Cursing. Crying. Hurt so bad, he started laughing. Made me laugh. Till his insides started spillin' out... Coughing blood on my face that I was too afraid to wipe off. I actin' like it don't hurt. *(He assumes his gang pose.)* Everybody gotta die sometime... Life goes on... Blood in, blood out, **sangre por sangre, carne de mi carne, vida por vida**... **Barrio**... Where you feel **bienvenido**... Wanted, **como en tu casa.** Think some math teacher's gonna cover my ass? Or give me the respect I get from my homeys? The pride? Not in this life. You wanna talk numbers? Three thousand gang deaths a year in the City of Angels—**Nuestra Señora la Reina de los Angeles.** You wanna talk math? Homes plus Homes plus Homes equals Strength. **Familia. Mi familia.** And you don't turn your back on that, ése. Not on blood. Not when it's your homey who's bleedin'. *That's* the truth, homes. *That's* education. *(Blackout.)*

SCENE FOUR

AT RISE: *Recess, a few weeks into the semester. STU-DENTS are goofing around in the hallway. PANCHO is near a door to the class as he and TITO check out CLAUDIA and some other GIRLS.*

PANCHO. Claudia thinks she's so hot just because she dates **gabachos.**

TITO. You *jealous*, man?

PANCHO. No, I mean, just 'cause she's fine, doesn't mean I want her.

TITO *(laughing)*. Oh, *man*. You're so full of shit! You *know* you dig her.

(ESCALANTE enters the hallway on his way to class. He spots the BOYS and casually strolls up beside PAN-CHO.)

PANCHO. *Shut up*, homes.

TITO. Yeah, well, just don't let her know. That's like the worst thing you can do with a woman.

ESCALANTE. You're in love, huh?

TITO *(laughing)*. He's buggin'.

ESCALANTE. Let me know...Which one?

PANCHO *(walking off)*. C'mon. Let's go.

ESCALANTE *(to TITO)*. How 'bout you, Johnny. C'mon, don't be afraid.

TITO *(laughing)*. I'm not Johnny, man. *(TITO walks off after PANCHO. ESCALANTE heads to his class.)*

ESCALANTE *(to himself)*. I know, Tito. Tito **el Grande.**

(TITO blasts his boombox. STUDENTS start dancing wildly. PRINCIPAL MOLINA and MRS. ORTEGA enter the hall. They're in the middle of a heated discussion.)

MOLINA *(entering)*. That's exactly the point I'm trying to make, Mrs. Ortega. *(To TITO.)* Tito, turn that thing off, or I'll confiscate it!

TITO *(turning off the box)*. It's recess. We're supposed to be relaxing.

MOLINA *(back to ORTEGA)*. I'll tell you now, I will not be the principal of the first school in the history of Los Angeles to lose its accreditation.

ORTEGA. I'm the last person to say that this school doesn't need to improve. But, if you want higher test scores, start by changing the economic level of this community.

(ESCALANTE re-enters the hall.)

ESCALANTE. Good morning, good morning. Excuse me, please, but I need more chalk for the classroom.

ORTEGA *(to MOLINA)*. As I said before, we lack the resources to implement the changes the district demands.

MOLINA. Yes, I know that, Mrs. Ortega. I also know that if we don't try *something*, we are certain to fail.

ESCALANTE. Forgive me, I'm sorry. I didn't mean to interrupt.

MOLINA. No, it's fine, Mr. Escalante. This is as good a time as any... Garfield High has been put on academic probation. If we don't turn things around this year, we'll lose our accreditation.

ORTEGA. If *we* fail. You can't teach logarithms to illiterates. Look, these kids come to us with barely a fifth grade education. There isn't a teacher in this school who isn't doing everything they possibly can.

ESCALANTE. I'm not. I could do more.

ORTEGA. I'm sure Mr. Escalante has good intentions, but he's only been here a short while.

ESCALANTE. If you treat them like losers, they act like losers. Hold them accountable, ask for more, and they will deliver.

MOLINA. You really think our students can do better?

ESCALANTE. Students will rise to the level of expectation, Señor Molina. *(Pause.)*

MOLINA. All right. What do you need, Mr. Escalante?

ESCALANTE. **Ganas**... That's all we need... **Ganas.**

(Offstage, we hear shouting and a crash—a fight is breaking out. CHUCO and a couple of the MARAVILLA GANG race across stage to join in. Some of the STUDENTS follow them out of curiosity. There are gunshots,

*and screams. Pandemonium. MOLINA chases after
CHUCO. ORTEGA huddles down in a corner. ESCA-
LANTE spots ANGEL racing across stage to join
CHUCO. ESCALANTE grabs him and puts him against
the wall.)*

ANGEL. Let go! Let go! *(ESCALANTE struggles to keep
ANGEL from escaping. He works him into an arm lock.
Offstage, a whistle blows. We hear the SECURITY
GUARDS shouting.)*

CHUCO *(offstage)*. Angel! ... Angel!

ANGEL. Let go! That's my homey! *(The offstage commo-
tion starts to die down. When it does, ESCALANTE finally loosens his grip on ANGEL. ORTEGA stands to
watch ESCALANTE confront ANGEL.)*

ESCALANTE. You need to hit someone, hit me, Mr. Ma-
nos de Piedra. *(ANGEL cocks his arm, but cannot bring
himself to hit ESCALANTE.)* You pretend not to hear,
Johnny, but I know you're listening. *(ANGEL storms
out. ORTEGA hands ESCALANTE the glasses he lost in
the scuffle.)*

ORTEGA. I think you're going to need more than just
ganas, Mr. Escalante. A lot more. *(She exits. ESCA-
LANTE looks around the halls and slowly heads into his
classroom. The school bell rings. The hallway empties of
STUDENTS.)*

*(The lights shift. ESCALANTE writes on his blackboard:
$1/4 + 1/4 = 2/4 = 1/2$. STUDENTS file into the classroom, laughing and chattering. There are about 20 kids
left. Some have dropped the class.)*

ESCALANTE. As soon as the bell rings from now on I want you in your seats ready for action. We will start each day with a quiz.

TITO. Oh, c'mon.

ESCALANTE. There will be no free rides, no excuses. Already have two strikes against you. Already behind. Have to play catch up. Take short cuts. Fast break on them. There are some people in this world who will assume that you know less than you do because of your name and complexion. But math is the great equalizer.

PANCHO. ... guy's dreamin' ...

ESCALANTE. Add and subtract, divide and conquer! When you go for a job the person giving you that job will not want to hear your problems, and neither do I. *(ESCALANTE strolls down the aisle. He thumps a sleeping CLAUDIA on the head. She snaps out of it.)* Hello, Señorita, you certainly have on a lot of makeup today. You have a contract with Dracula? *(PANCHO is reading a car magazine hidden in his notebook.)* Francisco García?

PANCHO *(with Anglicized pronunciation)*. It's Garcia.

ESCALANTE. Well, when I say García you answer, okay, Pancho? ... What you looking at García?

PANCHO. I'm not looking at nothing.

ESCALANTE. Okay. That's it. I warned you. No hot rod magazines in math class. *(ESCALANTE throws the magazine into the trash. He takes a tiny blue chair and places it in front of the STUDENTS. There's some heckling, laughter.)*

LUPE. Ooooo, we're in trouble now. *(More laughter.)*

ESCALANTE *(to PANCHO)*. Sit.

PANCHO. Me?

ESCALANTE. Nobody else.

PANCHO. No. I don't think so ...

CLAUDIA. Go on, Motorhead. *(More laughter, name calling. ESCALANTE moves from desk to desk, sometimes whispering, sometimes challenging, always inspiring.)*

ESCALANTE. I run the show. You're gonna do what I say. Don't do what I say, you gonna fly. Got other schools we can send you to. You won't like them. Gonna have to take three buses to get there. *(PANCHO considers this. Then, he clowns his way into the chair.)* Welcome to the show.

TITO. Some show. Can I get my money back? *(The KIDS laugh and begin to heckle PANCHO.)*

A FEW STUDENTS. Awwww. Look at the little baby in the chair! Where's your milk bottle? *(More laughter. A sign is hanging underneath the clock. It reads:* "Determination + Discipline + Hard Work = The Way to Success."*)*

ESCALANTE. Okay. Okay. See the sign? Goot. Read the sign ... Go on.

PANCHO. "Determination."

ESCALANTE. Determination means you *refuse* to quit. Never give up. Very goot. What else it say?

PANCHO. C'mon ...

A FEW STUDENTS. Ohhhh. What's the matter, baby, gotta go pee-pee? *(More laughter.)*

ESCALANTE. Better read quick.

PANCHO. "Discipline."

ESCALANTE. Discipline means you follow *instructions*. From your mom, your dad, your coach. I'm just a coach. And if you guys are my team, then I'm in big trouble. What else does it say? ... C'mon ...

PANCHO *(softly).* "Hard work."

ESCALANTE. Hard Work is the Future. *You* are the future. You can do it. Anybody can do...Then?...Let's go, Motorhead, not done yet.

PANCHO. "The way to success."

ESCALANTE. *Success.* Success means Victory. Does not come easily. Don't find it in box of Cracker Jacks. No. Too bad...Where do you find it? Huh? *(To ANA.)* Smart Lady, you know. Tell them, where do you find it? *(ANA looks down and shrugs her shoulders. ESCALANTE smiles.)* In *yourself.* Believe in yourself, you're gonna do it. Means you're building *confidence.* You're gonna do it. You're gonna do it, Johnny. You're the best...Now I got a new sign. Motorhead, go hang it up. *(ESCALANTE points to a rolled banner on his desk. PANCHO crosses to it and picks it up.)*

PANCHO. Where you want it?

ESCALANTE *(smiling).* You decide, Johnny. *(PANCHO stands on a chair and hangs one side of the banner. He moves the chair and hangs the other side. Over sign hanging:)* You're gonna work harder than you ever worked before. You need the tools. Gotta get good. Gonna have to practice. *(PANCHO jumps down and the banner unfurls. It reads:* GANAS—THAT IS ALL I NEED. *The STUDENTS cheer and clap sarcastically. PANCHO takes a bow. To PANCHO.)* Way to go, Johnny, now take your seat. *(PANCHO rolls back to his desk. ESCALANTE moves among the kids.)* You have entered Garfield but Garfield has not entered you. You are murderers. You kill time. Now—that's finished. You late, you get the chair. Don't come prepared—chair. miss class, you see The Principal. Don't like the rules, you fly. Easily understood? Good. In order to get good, there has to be *the desire*. The **Ganas**. That's the only thing I ask of you. *Ganas*. And a haircut. *(Tugs TITO's hair.)* If you don't have the **ganas** I will give it to you. Because I am an expert. Today is Monday, tomorrow is Wednesday, Friday is payday. The weekly test. There will be no diagonal vision. Eyes on your own paper. Cheating is not tolerated. *(ESCALANTE starts handing out quizzes. The STUDENTS groan.)*

TITO. You gotta be kidding!

ESCALANTE. You will have ten minutes to finish a quiz. You finish early, you work on whatever problem is on the board. No questions? Goot. *(The STUDENTS resign themselves to working on the quiz. ESCALANTE smiles.)* And you're not students anymore. This is Garfield High. That means you're *Bulldogs*. Dog-dog-dog-dog-dog-dog...

(ESCALANTE continues his chant, prowling the room as the STUDENTS work on the quiz. Enter CHUCO, ANGEL, and the MARAVILLA GANG. ESCALANTE stops his chant. Everyone stops working.)

TITO *(softly)*. The chair, give 'em the chair...

ESCALANTE *(to TITO)*. Okay, okay. *(To CHUCO.)* Are your friends auditing?

CHUCO. Yeah. I "audited" them to come with me.

ESCALANTE. You see? Safety in *numbers*. *(CHUCO does his strut and sits. ANGEL follows. The rest of the MARAVILLA GANG remains standing. No one works on their quiz. ESCALANTE takes off his tie and wraps it around his head like a gang member. He starts imitating the walk and talk of CHUCO.)* I am **"El Ciclón,"** from Bolivia. One man gang. This is *my* domain. **Pues ni modo.** *(In CHUCO's face.)* Don't give me no gas. I'll jump on your face. Tattoo your chromosomes. *(Some STUDENTS laugh. CHUCO ignores ESCALANTE. ESCALANTE resumes his own style. He crosses up to the board and erases the problem. He writes in its place: $-2 + 2 = ?$.)* Okay. This is basic math, but basic math is too easy, even for you **burros.** So, I'm going to teach you algebra, because I'm the champ. If the only thing you know how to do is add and subtract, you will only be prepared to do one thing. Pump gas—

CHUCO. Hey, ripping off a gas station is better than working in one, **que no?**

ANGEL. **Orale!** *(ANGEL and CHUCO shake hands, cholo-style.)*

ESCALANTE. **Orale!** I'm a tough guy. Tough guys don't do math. Tough guys deep-fry chicken for a living. Work at **Pollo Loco.** You want a wing or a leg, man?

TITO. I want a thigh. *(The STUDENTS laugh at CHUCO's expense.)*

ESCALANTE. **Orale.** Whoever heard of negative and positive numbers? Anybody?

PANCHO. Yeah, negative numbers are like unemployment. Ten million people out of work. That's a negative number.

ESCALANTE. We're gonna need a lot of Kleenexes. There's gonna be a lot of bloodshed here. *(To LUPE.)* You been to the beach?

LUPE. Yeah.

ESCALANTE *(to PANCHO)*. You ever play with the sand?

PANCHO. C'mon, man...

ESCALANTE *(to CHUCO)*. Finger Man! ... Come on, Finger Man, did you ever dig a hole? ... The sand that comes out of the hole, that's a positive. The hole ... is a negative. That's it. Simple. Anybody can do. Minus two plus two equals? *(To ANGEL.)* Hey, Nethead, how about you? **Orale!** Answer it. Come on, you know the answer. Minus two plus two. Fill the hole. What's that on your knuckles? *(The class has gotten very quiet. ESCALANTE holds up ANGEL's hands and reads the tattooed knuckles. Spelling it out.)* L-O-V-E H-A-T-E. If I had that on my hands I wouldn't raise them either. *(ESCALANTE gets next to ANGEL's ear. ANGEL just stares ahead.)* Hey, tough guy. **Orale!** Come on. Negative two plus two equals ... Anyone can do. Fill the hole. *(ANGEL is still. PANCHO snickers.)*

CHUCO. I don't think so, **ése.**

ESCALANTE. Come on, just fill the hole. You gonna let these **burros** laugh at you? Minus two plus two equals ... *(ANGEL turns his back to ESCALANTE.)* I'll break your neck like a toothpick. *(Makes crunching sound.)* **Orale.** Minus two plus two equals ... *(ANGEL continues to defy his teacher. ESCALANTE stays close to ANGEL's ear. He waits. ANGEL barely moves his mouth.)*

ANGEL. Zero.

ESCALANTE. Zero? You're right. Simple. That's it. *(ESCALANTE skips to the board and finishes the problem.)* Minus two plus two equals zero. He just filled the hole. Did you know that neither the Greeks nor the Romans were capable of using the concept of zero? It was your ancestors, the Mayans, who first contemplated the zero. The absence of value. True story. You **burros** have math in your blood.

ANGEL. Hey, Kimo Sabe **todo!** It's the Lone Ranger! The man knows everything! **Orale!** Kimo Sabe!

CHUCO. Kimo Sabe **nada!** *(CHUCO stands. Everything stops for a moment. CHUCO stares at ANGEL, then gestures to a door. Exiting.)* Angel! **Vámonos!** *(CHUCO heads out with his GANG in tow. ANGEL rises from his chair, reluctantly following.)*

ESCALANTE. Nice knowing you. Have a nice day. *Arrivederci! (The GANG has left except for ANGEL. He stops and looks to ESCALANTE.)*

ANGEL. Kimo Sabe **todo.** *(ESCALANTE watches ANGEL exit. A few STUDENTS repeat the nickname "Kimo Sabe.")*

(RAFAELA FUENTES enters.)

RAFAELA *(hesitantly).* I was said to go here.

ESCALANTE. Goot. Another customer... You're in luck. I've got two seats. Take your pick. Relax, take Sominex. Don't sleep in my class. I take that as an insult. *(The bewildered RAFAELA takes CHUCO's old desk. ESCALANTE looks at ANGEL's vacant spot and sighs. He writes a set of parenthesis on the board. He points to them, then fills in the equation: $-(-2) = +2$. Over the above:)* Okay! Parenthesis means multiply. Every time you see this, you multiply. A negative times a negative equals a positive... A negative times a negative equals a positive, say it. *(Silence.)* A negative times a negative equals a positive. Say it!

ANA. A negative times a negative equals a positive.

ESCALANTE. Again! *(Silence.)* There's beauty in silence. I like it. Okay. Everyone!

ANA & JAVIER. A negative times a negative equals a positive.

ESCALANTE. I can't hear you!

CLAUDIA, TITO, ANA & JAVIER. A negative times a negative equals a positive.

ESCALANTE. Louder!

THE WHOLE CLASS. A negative times a negative equals a positive.

ESCALANTE. Louder!

THE WHOLE CLASS *(louder)*. A negative times a negative equals a positive!

ESCALANTE *(with the STUDENTS)*. A negative times a negative equals a positive! A negative times a negative equals a positive! *(The refrain continues a few more times and then:)* Why? *(Lights fade to black as the STUDENTS ponder ESCALANTE's question.)*

SCENE FIVE

AT RISE: *A spot comes up on RAFAELA holding writing paper, an envelope and some photos. She sits at a desk and begins to write. In the background, light comes up on ESCALANTE, ANA and JAVIER. They are putting up Christmas decorations.*

RAFAELA *(halting English)*. Dear Mama. My teacher say to write always the English so to get good. *(She stops writing and addresses the audience.)* Takes many weeks before Mama gets letter in Guatemala. Then she needs carry letter to next town, whole day on bus. She pay

abogado 18 **quetzales** to read the English. Ten cars I need clean by hand so to mail three American dollars to Mama and make happy at how good is my English she hear in Spanish. **Loco**...Mama speak **Quiché** then she learn Spanish from the nuns. Until **mi abuelo** was killed by **un soldado** who steal his **burro.** Mama leave school so to cut the sugar cane. But she make promise to The Virgin, her child go to school even if the earthquake...."Work hard, speak the English, everyday be gifts and blessings. Better than home, much better"...Last thing Mama say before I come to **El Norte.** *(RAFAELA resumes writing the letter.)* Here for you is pictures of me and Teresita. Would you like dress like she wear? I lucky to be staying in house so nice. *(RAFAELA again confides in the audience.)* How I tell Mama that Teresita only talk about American dollars? She is left by husband alone. She say if I make no more contribution I am to go. So I pay more so Mama don't feel Teresita move me out because I was disrespect to her friend she have from when they were children. "Send Mama pictures of us on new sofa by Christmas tree," Teresita tell to me. *(Pointing at photo.)* This new sofa took away by Sears men because her plastic money run off. *(Another photo.)* We take photo in front of big car in Hollywood Boulevard that belong to long-haired man with guitar, not Teresita. Many things I do not understand in this strong country. Who in **mi pueblo** believe students paint ugly the school? Break the books? Point guns at teachers? Why someone not want something they get for free? *(RAFAELA resumes writing the letter.)* I am happy, Mama. I eat meat every day. I have luck to make many friends. It is always new thing I see and always I am thanking you

for the life I am making. All my love, and God watch
over you. Rafaela. *(She folds the letter and seals the envelope.)* **Con todo mi amor y que Dios te bendiga.**
*(Lights fade down on RAFAELA. In the blackout we
hear:)*

SECRETARY *(over P.A. system)*. Your attention, please.
All undocumented aliens who wish to remain in school
must have INS form 11E filled out and signed by a parent or guardian by Monday. *(The Secretary repeats the
message in Spanish.)*

SECRETARY *(over P.A. system)*. **Atención, por favor.
Todos los estudiantes extranjeros e indocumentados
que deseen permanecer en esta escuela deben llenar
el formulario once-E de Inmigración y traerlo fir-
mado por padre, madre o guardián legal a más tar-
dar el lunes próximo.**

*(The lights come up on ESCALANTE's classroom. It is
December, the end of a school day. The walls of the
classroom have more pictures of inspirational people
and Christmas decorations. ESCALANTE is grading papers in the classroom. ANGEL enters, making sure that
no one sees him do it. ESCALANTE looks up.)*

ESCALANTE. What's the matter, Johnny? You an empty set?
ANGEL. Hey, Kimo man, I want to talk to you about the
class. Y'know, maybe we can do a deal here—
ESCALANTE. You already lost your seat. Don't give me
no gas.
ANGEL. I know about that. That was a mistake. I'm gonna
play it straight with you, man. I got a little problem,
though.

ESCALANTE. Yeah. Me.

ANGEL. No, no, no, seriously, man. Books. Can't have the homeys see me haul them around.

ESCALANTE. You wouldn't want anyone to think you're intelligent, huh?

ANGEL. So, maybe I could have two books. Keep one stashed at home, huh? *(ESCALANTE goes to his desk drawer and takes out several books. He opens each and removes a small card.)*

ESCALANTE. I'll cut you a deal. I'll give you <u>three</u> books. One for class, one for home, and one for your locker. So people know you never take it out.

ANGEL. Hey, man, this one's broken. *(ESCALANTE replaces the broken book. He hands the cards to ANGEL.)*

ESCALANTE. Sign each.

ANGEL. What's this for?

ESCALANTE. That's how much the book cost. That's how much you pay if you mess me up, put in the graffiti. Easily understood?

ANGEL *(signs each of the cards)*. Yep.

ESCALANTE. So. What do I get?

CHUCO *(offstage)*. *Angel!!!*

ANGEL. Protection, Kimo ... **Protección** ... understand?

ESCALANTE. Yep. I understand ... I understand. *(ANGEL makes for an exit, stashing the books under his jacket. ESCALANTE remains in the classroom, humming to himself. Singing.)* On the first day of Christmas, a **cholo** came to me ...

(Enter ANA and her father, HÈCTOR DELGADO.)

ANA. Papa, this is Mr. Escalante, my math teacher.

ESCALANTE *(smiling)*. Mr. Delgado. How are you?

DELGADO. **Mucho gusto.**

ESCALANTE. To what do I owe this pleasure?

ANA. I can't stay in your class.

ESCALANTE. Why not?

ANA. My—

DELGADO. *Anita*... Señor Escalante, I have a family restaurant. Already she spends too much time studying. Now, with the extra work from your class, **imposible**... So. Señor Molina said we need your signature—

ESCALANTE. No way. I won't sign. Ana should stay in this class. She's top kid.

DELGADO. The restaurant needs her.

ESCALANTE. You should hire another waitress. Ana can be the first one in your family to graduate from high school. Go to college.

DELGADO. I thank you for your concern, Mr. Escalante. But, her mother works there, her sisters, her brothers. This is a family business. She has responsibilities.

ESCALANTE. What about responsibility to her future? She could help the family more by getting an education.

DELGADO. Ahhh, probably get married. She wouldn't finish college.

ANA. *Papa.*

DELGADO. *Ana!* **Espera afuera.** *(ANA is close to tears as she leaves the classroom. She waits in the hall as the MEN resume the debate.)*

ESCALANTE. She talks about going to medical school.

DELGADO. No. I don't think so.

ESCALANTE. She should make her own choices.

DELGADO. **Un momento! Yo soy el padre de la niña, no usted!**

ESCALANTE. She'll just get fat and stupid. She'll waste her life away in your restaurant. She's top kid!

DELGADO. I started washing dishes for a nickel an hour. Now, I own that restaurant. Did I waste my life?!

ESCALANTE. I washed dishes too, when I first came to this country. But that—

DELGADO. Good! Strap on an apron. Come by and give us a hand.

ESCALANTE *(overlapping)*. She could go to college, come back and teach you how to run the place.

DELGADO. Professor, I know how to run my own family! Now, please, the *signature. (Reluctantly, ESCALANTE signs the paper.)*

ESCALANTE. Mr. Delgado, you've obviously done well for your family. If you believe yourself to be a good father, you must believe you raised your daughter to make the right decisions on her own...Please sir, I just want what's best for Ana.

DELGADO. So do I, Mr. Escalante. So do I.

(The DELGADOS exit. Exhausted, ESCALANTE returns to his desk and packs up his papers. He turns off the classroom light and starts into the hallway. ARMANDO, the janitor, is sweeping the trash-filled hall.)

ARMANDO. You leaving, Mr. Escalante?

ESCALANTE. **Si,** Armando. My wife's gonna kill me. I'm already late for dinner.

ARMANDO. Oh, all right.

ESCALANTE. Why?

ARMANDO. No, that's okay. Never mind.

ESCALANTE. Hey, Armando. **Qué te pasa?**

ARMANDO. No, it's just, you see, I'm taking this night class so I can get my G.E.D. diploma? And I'm having a hard time with the math.

ESCALANTE. Math? I'm the champ. Let's see what you got, Johnny. *(ARMANDO pulls a piece of paper out of his pocket and hands it to ESCALANTE. ESCALANTE puts down his briefcase and takes a look at the paper.)* No problem. Piece of cake. *(Lights fade down on ESCA-LANTE and ARMANDO.)*

(Lights up on LUPE. She is kneeling down, praying. ES-CALANTE and ARMANDO are in the classroom taking down the Christmas decorations and hanging signs.)

LUPE. Dear Lord...It's me, again. I wanted to thank you for helping Mama get her new cleaning job at the convention center. Papa's not so happy that she's working nights, but now he can get that new grass blower, 'cause the old one was giving him kidney problems. Thank you for keeping Margarita safe when she ran into the street. I should have been paying more attention, but Tomás, Jose and Flaco were fighting, and there's just too many kids in one room... **Diosito Mio,** I know I should be happy with the way things are, but you're going to have to give me the strength of Mother Teresa so I can maintain my diet. Please, please, please, allow me not to fall into temptations like **carnitas de puerco,** french fries and all the **helado de chocolate** in your creation. Give me the tastes buds for the fruits and veggies that are gonna make me skinny in the eyes of this world. I guess it could be worse. I could be stupid and fat...Then, I wouldn't care about my hair, my clothes. I'd be too dumb

to notice if some guy was into me. Not like there are
any. Except, maybe Pancho...He likes me, he just don't
know it, yet. Not that I'm desperate or anything. But, it
would be nice to be close to someone...When you're
tired or depressed, somebody to hold onto...Would that
be okay with you? I understand the whole thing about
pre-marital sex, but **Diosito Mio,** does being a virgin
mean the only thing I can hug is my pillow?...I mean, I
could just fall asleep in his arms...Please watch over
Grandma, and Mama and Papa...Please make sure the
little monsters stay healthy and safe...Please forgive me
for always being such a smart-ass, I mean smart-mouth.
*(She begins to quietly say the "Our Father" in Spanish.
As she prays, the lights fade to black.)*

SCENE SIX

AT RISE: *It is January. ESCALANTE, ARMANDO, and the
Christmas decorations are gone. On the walls, more inspirational slogans:* "What is mediocre is useless," "If
you've tried to do something and failed, you are much
better off than if you had tried to do nothing and succeeded." *The STUDENTS are hanging out in the classroom. Some of them are eating lunch. A few are tossing
a ball around, others are just goofing off. The room has
become a safe haven for them. In one corner, JAVIER
and ANA are going over an assignment together. RA-
FAELA sits by herself. TITO and PANCHO are off together. TITO is playing an instrument and singing.
LUPE and CLAUDIA are on the other side of the room,
fixing their makeup.*

TITO. Pancho, man, you're always checking out Claudia.

PANCHO. You know that's the only reason I'm still in Kimo's class.

TITO *(sings)*. Pancho's in love ...

PANCHO. Shut up, shh, man, shit! She's looking over here.

CLAUDIA *(looks over to PANCHO and TITO)*. Look at Pancho. Slobbering like a dog.

LUPE *(turns away fast when she sees PANCHO looking their way)*. Shh, quiet! I think he heard you!

CLAUDIA. Jesus, girl, don't tell me you're into Pancho Villa.

LUPE. Don't embarrass me, **Camejo.**

CLAUDIA. Come on, don't be shy, talk to him. *(CLAUDIA starts toward the BOYS, LUPE slowly joins her. They saunter over to TITO and PANCHO. CLAUDIA breaks the ice.)* I'm pretty fed up with that **pelón** we got for a teacher.

PANCHO. Yeah, Escalante's got a real bug up his butt, giving us homework over vacation. *(PANCHO nudges TITO.)*

TITO. Oh, yeah. He's from Bolivia, South America, man. Probably some Nazi come out of hiding or something.

PANCHO *(begins to mimic ESCALANTE's walk and talk)*. Whatsamatter, Johnny, you don't like my class? Too bad. Go work for Burger King.

(A few more STUDENTS enter the classroom. There are about 14 now, only the core group remains.)

LUPE. Don't you guys know what's happening? Garfield's losing its accreditation.

PANCHO. So only teachers who act like assholes are gonna keep their jobs.

CLAUDIA. Well, what if we all decide not to take his tests? I mean, he can't fail the whole class.

TITO. Mutiny? That's cool. *(The CONSPIRATORS nod and smile. They whisper their plans to the rest of the class.)*

PANCHO *(imitating ESCALANTE)*. Okay, Johnny! You do the work or you take a hike because I am The Champ! Dog-dog-dog-dog ...

(ESCALANTE enters. PANCHO doesn't see him but the others do. Everyone finds a seat. PANCHO finally sees ESCALANTE, and tries to cover his embarrassment. Sheepishly, he heads to a desk. ESCALANTE smiles at PANCHO.)

ESCALANTE *(handing out tests)*. Welcome back! Happy New Year! You're still failing! Got your algebra test results. We don't do better today, heads are gonna roll.

JAVIER *(looks at his test grade)*. I've never gotten anything lower than a B+ in my life.

ESCALANTE. Because you take those Mickey Mouse classes. Always get an A. Here you got another chance to do a solid D. All right, let's see the homework. *(Some STUDENTS groan. ESCALANTE hands out a stack of new quizzes. The STUDENTS pass them around. ESCALANTE moves from student to student, collecting homework.)* Okay, first quiz. New semester, new rules. Today you got *five* minutes. Gotta hurry, running outta time. Gotta move faster. *(The MUTINEERS look to each other for the signal. PANCHO looks over to CLAUDIA and grins.)*

PANCHO *(whispering)*. Here he comes.

LUPE *(whispering)*. Watch this. *(LUPE launches the mutiny by turning her quiz over. CLAUDIA does the same. PANCHO, TITO and a bunch of OTHERS follow along. ESCALANTE goes to LUPE.)*

ESCALANTE. You finished already?

LUPE. I'm not taking the test.

ESCALANTE *(softly)*. What's the matter with you? You didn't turn in your homework, either.

LUPE. My goat ate it. *(CLAUDIA, PANCHO, TITO and a few OTHERS laugh.)*

ESCALANTE. You don't do your homework, you don't get a ticket to watch the show.

JAVIER. Give her the chair! *(ESCALANTE takes out the chair.)*

LUPE. No way.

ESCALANTE. The longer you wait, the longer you sit.

JAVIER & A FEW OTHERS *(softly)*. Chair, chair, chair...

LUPE. Come on, you guys!

HALF THE CLASS. Chair, chair, chair! *(LUPE looks around at her fellow MUTINEERS, but they offer her no support.)*

ESCALANTE. Either you get in the chair or you fly. Lots of things you can do. Sombrero weaving, making license plates. Your choice.

MOST OF THE CLASS *(louder)*. Chair! Chair! Chair!

LUPE. Shit. *(To a chorus of* "Chair!" *LUPE finally gets up and sits in the blue chair.)*

VARIOUS STUDENTS. Ha, ha. That's what you get. You're the show!

LUPE. Shut up.

ESCALANTE. Anybody else not doing the quiz, I got plenty of chairs... All right, back to work. You don't have much time left. *(ALL turn their quizzes right side up and begin working. Softly to LUPE.)* See, now you're the show. *(ESCALANTE briefly prowls the aisles, then returns to LUPE's side.)* What's the matter with you? You're top kid. Come on, you're the best! You're gonna have to take the quiz anyway. You're in quarantine. Back here, 3 o'clock. Go on, back to your seat. *(LUPE obeys and is heckled back to her seat. On passing PAN-CHO, she whacks him on the head. ESCALANTE writes a problem on the board while the class works on the quiz.)*

(ANGEL, sans hair net, tries to slip into the room.)

SCATTERED VOICES. Late, late, late...

ESCALANTE. Whoa, no way, Angel. No chair for you. Go find yourself a Mickey Mouse class. Go to woodshop, make yourself a shoeshine box. You're gonna need it. *(The STUDENTS heckle ANGEL. He walks to the front of the class.)*

ANGEL. Okay, Kimo. You're the man, you know best... Why don't you put them all in college, huh? Then let dumb taco benders like me pick their vegetables for them, collect their garbage, clip their poodle's toenails.

ESCALANTE. You're off the team. Goodbye. Have a nice day. *(ANGEL throws his hands up and backs into the blackboard, taking the pose of Christ on the cross.)*

ANGEL. I may be a sinner, but, I'm willin' to pay for my sins... *(Some laughter. Everyone waits to see what ES-CALANTE will do.)*

ESCALANTE. Okay, one shot deal. See you at 3 o'clock. Make-up quiz. Sit down. *(As ANGEL heads to his desk he flashes his tattooed knuckles in PANCHO's face.)*

PANCHO. Get out of my face.

ANGEL. I got more bad news for you, profes. Now, I know what I'm gonna say is really gonna trip you out, but I expect you to take it like a man... Mr. Escalante, I forgot my pencil. *(The class breaks into laughter. RAFAELA hands ANGEL a pencil.)*

ESCALANTE. Okay, time is up. Pass 'em forward. Thank you, thank you, thank you. Everyone look at the board. Will someone please read for me this problem? Anybody? *(ESCALANTE collects the quizzes and puts them on his desk.)*

STUDENTS *(in unison)*. Juan has five times as many girlfriends as Pedro. Carlos has one girlfriend less than Pedro. If the total number of girlfriends between them is 20, how many does each gigolo have? *(The STUDENTS laugh. ESCALANTE roams the aisles. The STUDENTS can't take their eyes off him. JAVIER and TITO raise their hands.)*

ESCALANTE. Okay, okay. How many girlfriends does each gigolo have? Anybody? *(To TITO.)* Think you got it, Einstein? Do you think you're gonna do it?

TITO. Juan is x, Carlos is y. Pedro is x plus y. Is Pedro bisexual, or what? *(STUDENTS laugh and snicker.)*

ESCALANTE. I have a terrible feeling about you, Tito. **Camejo,** stand and deliver!

CLAUDIA. 5x equals Pedro's girlfriends?

ESCALANTE. You're pretty now, but you're gonna end up barefoot and pregnant, in the kitchen. *(He imitates a*

plane flying and crashing with his hand and voice.)
Yeooow!! ... Dog-dog-dog-dog ...

CLASS *(picking up chant)*. Dog-dog-dog-dog-dog-dog-dog ...

(PRINCIPAL MOLINA and MRS. ORTEGA enter. They look around the room.)

ANGEL. Late, late, late.

ESCALANTE *(overlapping)*. Okay, okay, okay, okay. How many girlfriends? What's the answer? *(MOLINA and ORTEGA take seats in the back.)*

PANCHO *(guessing)*. Subtract Carlos from Pedro and divide by Juan?

ESCALANTE *(squeaky voice)*. Some of these kids are in love, they're going to need heart transplants. Make me look bad in front of the boss.

RAFAELA. Can you have negative girlfriends?

ESCALANTE. No. Just negative boyfriends. *(As if to God.)* Forgive them for they know not what they do!

ANGEL. Carlos has x minus 5 girlfriends, **qué no?**

ESCALANTE. **"Qué no?"** is right, **qué no.** *(Some laughter. LUPE raises her hand.)* The answer to my prayers! Yes?

LUPE. May I go to the restroom, please? *(Laughter.)*

ESCALANTE. Hold it. You got two minutes. *(To JAVIER.)* Señor Maya? My job is in your hands. Hit it.

JAVIER. It's a trick question, Mr. Kimo. You can't solve it unless you know how many girlfriends they have in common. Right?

ESCALANTE *(to MOLINA and ORTEGA)*. It's not that they're stupid. It's just that they don't know anything.

(The kids laugh. ANA enters the room unbeknownst to ESCALANTE. She studies the problem on the board.)

JAVIER. I'm wrong? *(ESCALANTE attacks him with mock karate chops to the head.)*

ANA. X equals Pedro's girlfriends. 5x equals Juan's girlfriends. X minus 1 equals Carlos' girlfriends. X plus 5x plus x minus 1 equals 20, so, x equals 3. *(The class applauds. ANA smiles and sits.)*

ESCALANTE *(to ANA)*. Good to see you.

PANCHO. Hey, Kimo, this stuff makes no sense half the time. You gotta show us how it works in the real world.

ESCALANTE *(to MOLINA)*. Do you think it would be possible to get a couple of gigolos for a practical demonstration? *(The STUDENTS laugh.)* No, no, no, just kidding, just kidding. *(The bell rings and STUDENTS file out. ESCALANTE catches up with ANA.)* Your father changed his mind?

ANA. I told him if he didn't let me come to your class I would get pregnant before my 18th birthday. He bought me a desk so I can study at the restaurant!

ESCALANTE. That'll do it.

ANA. **Hasta mañana!** *(ESCALANTE smiles and shakes his head as ANA exits. He returns to his desk. ORTEGA and MOLINA walk over.)*

ESCALANTE. So. Do I pass the test?

MOLINA. You have some unusual methods, Mr. Escalante.

ESCALANTE. Thank you very much.

ORTEGA. But are they learning?

ESCALANTE *(opens his briefcase and takes out some papers)*. Their algebra midterms. *(Putting them down.)* B+, A-, B, C+, A-, B-, C, B+, A, A, A ...

ORTEGA. This is just one class.

ESCALANTE. I want to teach calculus next year.

MOLINA. What, you're leaving us, Kimo? You got a college job?

ESCALANTE. No. Here. I want to teach calculus to this class.

MOLINA *(chuckling)*. Calculus? Oh boy, that's a jump.

ORTEGA. That's ridiculous. They haven't had trig or math analysis.

ESCALANTE. They can take them both during the summer.

ORTEGA. You expect our best students to go to summer school?

ESCALANTE. From seven to 12...Every day, including Saturdays. Yep. That'll do it.

ORTEGA. Out of the question.

MOLINA. Our summer classrooms are reserved for remedial courses.

ESCALANTE. Mr. Molina, if you want to turn this school around you're gonna have to start from the top. You have to motivate them every minute, every day, even the best students.

ORTEGA. Mr. Escalante, please don't lecture us. I've been teaching here for 15 years, I think I know our students better than—

ESCALANTE *(interrupting)*. We're not teaching the right stuff!

ORTEGA. Our kids can't *handle* calculus. We don't even have the books.

ESCALANTE. Books are not the problem. I'll teach Bolivian-style. Students copy from the board. Step by step. Inch by inch, I'll mimeograph pages from a college text.

MOLINA. *College* calculus?!

ESCALANTE. Of course. They can take the Advanced Placement Test. Get college credit.

ORTEGA. There are some *teachers* who would have trouble passing the Advanced Placement Test.

MOLINA. You really think you can make this fly? *(Pause.)*

ESCALANTE. I teach calculus next year, or, have a good day.

ORTEGA *(to MOLINA)*. Well, if this man can walk in here and dictate his own terms over my objections, I see no reason for me to continue as department chair.

MOLINA. Raquel, you're taking this far too personally—

ORTEGA *(interrupting)*. I am thinking about those kids! Fewer than 2 percent of the seniors in this entire country even attempt the A.P. tests. This isn't Andover or Exeter...If our kids try and don't succeed, you'll shatter what little self-confidence they do have. These aren't the types that bounce back...Have a good day. *(ORTEGA exits. Pause.)*

MOLINA. You've got a way of putting people off...

ESCALANTE. The truth can do that...

MOLINA. Jaime, has it occurred to you that she may be right? Kids are dropping your class already. And now you want them to give up summer vacation?

ESCALANTE. Hugo, if my kids can pass the Advanced Placement Test, they'll get college credit. Be a big plus for your school. For the whole community. *(ESCALANTE collects his belongings. MOLINA sighs.)*

MOLINA. Are you sure these kids will go to summer school?

ESCALANTE. Yep.

MOLINA. I certainly hope you're right. *(MOLINA exits, leaving ESCALANTE alone onstage. Lights fade down.)*

SCENE SEVEN

AT RISE: *Lights fade up on the first day of summer school. It is early in the day and already it's oppressively hot. The classroom now has pictures of the space shuttle and Mayan pyramids. The newest incentive banner reads: "Calculus wasn't meant to be easy. It already is." ESCA-LANTE is onstage alone, waiting. He checks his watch and then crosses over to the air conditioner. He tinkers with the controls. Nothing. Frustrated, he gives it a kick. It starts momentarily, then dies abruptly. ESCALANTE draws a circle and then a cross inside it, so it looks like a pie with four slices. He writes the letters S, A, C, T, one in each section, starting in the top left section, moving clockwise. Next to the S he writes: Sin +. Next to the A: All +. Beside the C: Cos +, and next to the T: Tan +. Then, in big letters, the phrase:* All Seniors Turn Crazy! *Some of this can occur underneath the following dialogue. ARMANDO enters.*

ARMANDO. I made sure the gate was unlocked.

ESCALANTE. **Muchas gracias.** *(ESCALANTE checks his watch.)*

ARMANDO. It's tough to get kids in school during the summer.

ESCALANTE. They still got one minute.

(ANGEL enters.)

ANGEL. Hey, Kimo. You proud of me? I'm the first dude here. *(Pointing to the sign.)* What's calcoolus?

ARMANDO *(correcting ANGEL).* It's *calculus. (ARMANDO exits.)*

(JAVIER and ANA come running in, out of breath.)

JAVIER. Sorry we're late, Kimo. We thought we'd give everybody else a head start. *(They see the empty classroom. ESCALANTE smiles at them as they take two desks up front.)*

(A few more STUDENTS trickle in. They all open their notebooks. ANA looks around at the empty desks. TITO, CLAUDIA and a few other STUDENTS come running in.)

ESCALANTE. You're late.
TITO. By whose clock? *(They're frozen at the doors, waiting to see if ESCALANTE will let it slide.)*

(PANCHO and LUPE have entered the hallway holding hands. They stop in front of the classroom and kiss gently.)

ESCALANTE. My class, my clock. Everyone, synchronize the watches: Now. 8:01 and 29 seconds. *(ESCALANTE smiles and everyone laughs as they take their seats.)* All right, let's go. Plenty of good seats left. Hey, where's Motorhead?
CLAUDIA *(slyly).* He's with Lupe. *(ESCALANTE makes his way to the door. When he spots the kissing COUPLE, he motions for a few kids to come watch. Soon there is a small cluster watching LUPE and PANCHO kiss.)*

ESCALANTE. Careful. You can make babies from doing that. Just kidding, just kidding. *(Everyone breaks out laughing, including ESCALANTE as they pile back into their desks. ESCALANTE gives PANCHO a swat on his way past.)*

(RAFAELA knocks gently and enters.)

RAFAELA. Excuse me, Kimo. I sell oranges on freeway ramp. There was accident, traffic slow down, lots of business. *(ESCALANTE waves her in and she takes her seat, passing out oranges on the way.)*

ESCALANTE. Okay, okay. Sit down. Do you think I want to do this? The Japanese pay me to do this. They're tired of making *everything*. They want you guys to pull your own weight. So they can take vacations on Mount Fuji.

CLAUDIA. Kimo, it stinks in here.

ESCALANTE. Somebody give Claudia an orange. *(She is quickly surrounded by outstretched hands, each holding an orange. ESCALANTE refers to the board.)* All right, here's a shortcut for you **burros**, so you remember what's positive in which quadrant. Here, *All* are positive; here, *Sine* is positive; here, *Cosine;* here, *Tangent.* Got it? No? What's the matter? You lost? Don't like summer school? You think this is bad? You guys have it easy! *(Melodramatically.)* When I was your age, one day on my way to school I got lost in the hot, steamy Amazonian jungle. It was 120 degrees. I started hallucinating, wandering in circles, within the grasp of **los animales salvajes.** *(Collapsing to the floor.)* To keep my sanity, I said this axiom, over and over in my head, until I was able to claw my way back to civilization. All Seniors

Turn Crazy... All Seniors Turn Crazy... *(Referring to the board.)* All, Sine, Cosine, Tangent. *All Seniors Turn Crazy...* A-S-T-C. A-S-T-C!! If it wasn't for trigonometry, none of us would be here now. *(The KIDS applaud ESCALANTE's performance. He stands up and takes a bow, then crosses to the board.)*

ANGEL. Kimo, I thought this room was supposed to have an air conditioner, man.

ESCALANTE. It does have an air conditioner. Just doesn't work.

ANGEL. Great.

ESCALANTE. You should think, *cool*, man. Think... like a cool calculus team. Think... *(Slowly the class fills in the blank.)*

STUDENTS *(in unison)*. ... cool...

ESCALANTE. Think...

STUDENTS *(in unison)*. Cool... *(ESCALANTE mouths the word, "Think," and gestures for them to continue. Soothingly:)* Cool ... Cool ... Cool ... Cool ... cool ... *(The lights fade to black.)*

END OF ACT ONE

ACT TWO
Senior Year

(In the blackout we hear:)

SECRETARY'S VOICE *(over P.A. system)*. On behalf of the principal and the faculty, we'd like to welcome you back from summer vacation. Anyone caught smoking on school property may face suspension. Also, for safety reasons, it is advised that female students should only use the restrooms in pairs. Please make sure to inform your teachers that you need accompaniment and they will provide the proper hall passes. Thank you.

(The Secretary repeats the announcement in Spanish as the lights come up on the beginning of the new school year.)

SECRETARY'S VOICE *(over P.A. system)*. **En nombre del director y la facultad deseamos darle la bienvenida a un nuevo año escloar. El que sea agarrado fumando será suspendido. Por motivos de seguridad recomendamos que las estudiantes femeninas no vayan al baño solas. Infórmenle a sus maestros que necesitan un acompañante y ellos les darán el permiso requerido. Muchas gracias.**

(The hallway is filled with the usual pandemonium. Kids smoking, listening to music, clusters of GIRLS and BOYS scoping each other out. CHUCO and the MARAVILLA GANG are gathered off to one side. One of the GANG is spray painting their placa on a wall. ANGEL enters, reading from his class schedule. CHUCO spots him.)

CHUCO. **Orale!** *Homes...(ANGEL stops when he sees CHUCO and the GANG. ANGEL puts away his class schedule as CHUCO waves him over.)* Where you been, man? All summer, hide and seek with you.

ANGEL. Been busy...What you doing here? Thought you dropped out.

CHUCO *(smiling)*. Yeah, well, thought I'd pay a little visit to the school. *(CHUCO takes the schedule from ANGEL's pocket and looks it over.)* Oh, man. You still in Kimo's class? That **pelón** has you goin' good...You should dump this math shit and come hang out with **la clica,** get stoned, cruise Whittier. *(He puts the schedule back in ANGEL's pocket and fixes ANGEL's collar.)*

ANGEL. Yeah. Maybe.

CHUCO *(gives ANGEL a long, hard look)*. What's with this maybe shit? Man, we're **carnalitos**...**Mi misma sangre.**

ANGEL. We're still blood, homes. *(They shake hands, cholo-style.)*

CHUCO. Okay, so listen, bro, I got a little business to take care of. Why don't you keep an eye out for me, okay? *(CHUCO takes out some drugs and shows them to ANGEL.)*

ANGEL. Man, you can't be selling that shit here.

CHUCO. Just take a second—

ANGEL. No way, ése, no way.

CHUCO. What's the **pinche** fuck with you, bro?

ANGEL. The principal will have my little **culito** on the street, homes.

CHUCO (*stares down ANGEL*). What's the matter, **Mamasita?** ... (*ANGEL looks at CHUCO and shakes his head. Almost the entire MARAVILLA GANG is watching.*) C'mon, **tirame un beso**. (*ANGEL turns to walk away. CHUCO shoves him from behind and ANGEL falls to the ground. His pencil falls from behind his ear to the floor beside him. ANGEL picks it up in a threatening manner.*) What's the matter, **puto**? Gonna stab me with a pencil? Not man enough to use a knife? ... (*A small CROWD has gathered, looking for a duel. ANGEL thinks about fighting, then breaks the pencil with one hand. He gets up and walks away, ignoring CHUCO.*) Where you going? Come back! ... Angel? ... *Angel!!*

(*CHUCO watches as ANGEL walks off. Upstage, there is a crash of breaking glass and some screaming and shouting. A MARAVILLA GANG MEMBER comes racing down the hall, a SECURITY GUARD not far behind. CHUCO and the rest of the GANG tear out through the audience, laughing and screaming. ESCALANTE enters.*)

GANG MEMBER. Welcome back, **pelón!!** (*The GANG MEMBER crashes into ESCALANTE while trying to escape. The SECURITY GUARD catches the GANG MEMBER and takes him off in handcuffs.*)

(*ESCALANTE collects his books, dusts himself off, and enters the classroom. The desks have been rearranged into clusters. He writes on the blackboard: A.P. Calculus. CLAUDIA, RAFAELA, and TITO all spill into the classroom. JAVIER, ANA and the rest of the class make their way in. ANGEL comes in last. While the rest of the school appears unchanged, there is a bit more enthusiasm within ESCALANTE's group. By now however, there are more desks than STUDENTS.)*

ESCALANTE *(overlapping entrances).* Welcome back, welcome back. Everybody still alive, that's a plus. You're still failing, though. *(STUDENTS groan and laugh. ESCALANTE moves amongst them playfully.)* Remember the good times we had over the summer? Remember trigonometry? Math analysis? Do you remember when things were really jumpin' good, oh yeah. Well, the good times are gone with the wind. It's now the good, the bad and the ugly. *(The class groans. ESCALANTE takes out a stack of forms and passes them out.)* We'll go step by step: Inch by inch. Calculus was not made to be easy. It already is.

JAVIER *(reading form).* Oh, come on! Contracts? You mean you can't trust us by now?

ESCALANTE. For those of you making the commitment, you will be preparing yourselves for the Advanced Placement Test. Make sure a parent or guardian signs it before you come to class tomorrow.

TITO. Wait, wait, wait. We have to come an hour before school, take your classes two periods, and stay until five?

ESCALANTE. Believe it or don't.

PANCHO. Saturdays? We have to come on Saturdays? *(PANCHO looks at the contract long and hard, then puts his head on his desk.)*

LUPE. And no vacations?

ESCALANTE. Yep. If you want to be on the calculus team.

ANGEL. **Orale,** Kimo! This is worse than juvy.

TITO. Kimo, we're seniors. This is supposed to be our year to slack off.

ESCALANTE *(tugs at TITO's hair)*. What's the matter, Johnny? Think you won't be able to make it Saturday morning after playing in your band Friday nights?

TITO. Look, you love scarin' us into doing stuff, Kimo, I know. But that gets old real fast.

ESCALANTE. Hey, Motorhead? What about you?

PANCHO *(looks up from his desk)*. Kimo, I don't want to let you down, but I gotta put school on hold.

ESCALANTE. What're you talking about?

PANCHO. My uncle offered me a job operating a forklift on Saturdays and Sundays. I'll be making time and a half.

ESCALANTE. So what?

PANCHO. So, two years in the union and I'll be making more than you. I'll be able to buy a new Trans Am.

ESCALANTE. Can't cruise through life, Pancho. Wouldn't you rather design cars than repair them? Can't even do that if they got fuel injection. Cars get old. Jobs come and go. An education lasts forever. Get it signed.

PANCHO. Kimo, I can't—

ESCALANTE *(tosses a clown's mask over to PANCHO)*. For you, Johnny. For when you work at Jack-in-the-Box. Fit right in.

PANCHO *(tosses the mask to the floor)*. Man, you're not gonna strip my gears. *(PANCHO walks out.)*

ESCALANTE. Anybody else jumping ship? Okay, let's go.

(The KIDS all eye each other for a moment and then slowly open up their notebooks. The bell rings to signal the start of class. Lights fade to a transition. The STU-DENTS spill out of the class and down the halls. LUPE and CLAUDIA enter the hallway. CLAUDIA is reading from a book.)

CLAUDIA. Originally referred to as *the* calculus by Sir Isaac Newton—

LUPE. The calculus? Sounds like a disease.

CLAUDIA. It says he invented it so he could figure out planet orbits, but he never bothered to tell anybody about his discovery.

LUPE. So how they know he discovered it?

CLAUDIA. 'Cause this other guy went around claiming *he* had invented it. But this guy was so stupid, he got it all wrong. So Newton had to go public and correct all his mistakes...

LUPE. For a genius, Newton was an idiot.

CLAUDIA. Yeah. I mean if I invented something I'd make sure everybody knew about it. That way I'd get paid. *(They laugh and LUPE tosses the book aside. CLAUDIA takes out her contract and looks at it.)*

LUPE. I can't believe we just lost summer vacation, and now Kimo wants us to come in morning, noon, and night.

CLAUDIA. My mom already thinks I'm crazy...She says, "Boys don't like you if you're too smart." She's never gonna sign this contract.

(PANCHO enters. He's still brooding.)

LUPE. You gonna come back to class, or what?

PANCHO. I don't know. My uncle's doing me a *favor*.

LUPE (*sidles up to him and strokes his back patiently*). But that job will always be there for you.

PANCHO. No, it won't! He'll hire somebody else! Man, Kimo's messin' up my plans.

LUPE. But I thought we were going to go to college together. (*LUPE strokes PANCHO's face. He pulls away.*)

PANCHO. Lupe, don't tell me what to do. I don't need you to think for me.

LUPE. I was just tryin to help—

PANCHO. Maybe I don't want your help, okay? (*LUPE turns and walks away.*) Oh, come on. Lupe! (*PANCHO stops her before she can exit. They talk silently upstage. A spot comes up on CLAUDIA, off by herself.*)

CLAUDIA. Pancho. He doesn't even know how good he's got it with Lupe. She's perfect for him. And all he can think about is what he doesn't have. Men think they're so smart 'cause they run everything, but really, they're just plain stupid. And they don't even realize it. Like, like what're those dogs called, the ones that hunt birds? ... They bark and bark, running around chasing after the bird, then, when they finally catch it—they spit it out. And then they start running around again, barking and shit, wondering what happened to the bird. (*She looks over at PANCHO and LUPE. They have made up and are hugging.*) Men. Sometimes I wish I didn't think they were so sexy. Like if I was into girls or something. At least I can understand them. I mean, this guy I was dating once? He didn't like to mess around before he played basketball. Said he had to channel himself or something. And that's cool, except, if the team lost a game? Then he'd wanna go at it *hot and heavy.* 'Cause he was gettin' his energy flowing the *right* way. One day he's *blocked*, next time he's *flowing*. Like a toilet or something. If he hadn't been such a good kisser, I woulda never put up with his crap. *Stupid.* Bark, bark, boss, boss. Always giving orders, making rules ... I'm sick of it. All the pushing ... Is it genetic or something? Guys have genes that make them assholes? ... My stepfather doesn't like dinner, so he yells at my mom. He gets drunk at night and yells some more. You try and say something to him, make some sense, and *smack*. Like it's a game or something. "Shut up or I'll smack ya," so I shut up and get smacked anyway. Smacking, barking, pushing. Almost wish I was a guy, so I could smack him around. But like, I want to be like that? *Please.* Nobody has the right to push anybody around. That might work with my mom, but not me. Told him that right to his face. I am woman, hear me roar. I'm gonna be somebody. I can take care of myself. I'll sign my own *contracts.* I'll make my own way. Get my own place. Where nobody's yelling and nobody's pushing and nobody's getting hit ... Someplace where *I* make the rules ... You don't like them? Fine. You can split ... It'll be a peaceful place. Somewhere a woman can relax ... And be happy ... And be safe ... And not have to hide from no dumb-ass dog that don't know no better than to leave the birds alone. (*CLAUDIA looks down at the contract. She forges a signature on the contract and puts it in her pocket. Lights fade down on her and up on the classroom.*)

(*It is 7 a.m. ESCALANTE is alone in the room, preparing for early morning class. He takes out a tape player, puts on some classical music and then crosses to the board. He writes out a problem. ARMANDO is mopping the hallway. ANA, JAVIER and TITO wander in. TITO is practically sleepwalking.)*

ARMANDO. What're you doing here so early?

ANA. Mr. Escalante's class, remember? *(ARMANDO nods his head. ANA and JAVIER head to the classroom. TITO wanders down the hall.)*

ARMANDO. Yo, Tito. Wrong way, man.

TITO. What?... Oh... Thanks. *(TITO heads toward the class.)*

(OTHER STUDENTS are filtering in. Because of the early hour, they are less than enthusiastic. ESCALANTE is waiting by the door receiving contracts from the STUDENTS as they enter.)

ESCALANTE. Thank you, thank you very much. You don't got it signed, you don't get a ticket to watch the show. Thank you, Mr. Kung Fu. *(To TITO.)* Hey, get a haircut, one more time I gotta tell you. Good morning, good morning. Mr. Blue Eyes, thank you very much. Elizabeth, my Taylor! Sophia, my Loren! Red, get a new jacket. Thank you, very much. *(To ANGEL.)* Clint, forget your gun? *(ANGEL hands him his contract.)* Unfold it. Good. *(Everyone has returned except for PANCHO. ESCALANTE puts the contracts in his briefcase and heads to the blackboard.)* Hey, how come it's so quiet?

JAVIER. It's 7 a.m., Kimo.

LUPE. Yeah, my rooster's still sleeping.

ESCALANTE. Okay, you see this problem on the board? *(ESCALANTE points to the board. No reaction from the*

STUDENTS.) Come on, *wake up,* drink coffee. You see this? One, you got the graph, right here. Two, this is it. The most important part. This, right here. It's a radius of rotation. That's it. Anybody got any questions? Anybody can do it... *(ESCALANTE prowls the room. ANGEL raises his hand and points out a sleeping TITO.)* As long as you remember one basic element, and that is—the element of surprise. *(He thwacks TITO on the head with a small red pillow. TITO awakens with a start.)* Stay awake! I take it personally. Oh, you're waking up, good morning! How are you? Bring toothpicks to pinch your eyes open. Easily understood, Johnny?

TITO *(still sleepy).* Me and my band were swimming with dolphins, whispering imaginary numbers, lookin' for the fourth dimension...

ESCALANTE. That's good. That's very good. Go back to sleep. Okay... *(Scattered laughs. TITO puts his head down on the pillow.)*

(PANCHO enters and ESCALANTE stops teaching. PANCHO drops off his signed contract on the desk and takes his seat. ESCALANTE has a smile on his face.)

PANCHO. What you smilin' about?

ESCALANTE. Who me? It's a beautiful morning. I love the morning. *(ESCALANTE takes in the ragged group. He turns off the music coming from his tape player.)* Hey! What're you gonna do, sleep while Rome's burning? Let's go. Wake up! Yeooowww!! Dog-dog-dog... *(ESCALANTE bounces around the room. The STUDENTS halfheartedly respond.)*

STUDENTS. Dog-dog-dog-dog ... *(ESCALANTE heads back to the blackboard. The STUDENTS continue the chant. ESCALANTE turns to them with a scowl.)*

ESCALANTE. Okay, okay. Enough fun. Back to work. *(The class groans. The lights fade out.)*

SCENE TWO

AT RISE: *Lights up. Most of the STUDENTS are still in their desks, working hard. Some are hanging up the Christmas decorations. ESCALANTE is quietly helping a couple of them off to one side. A bell rings signifying the end of the school day. We hear PRINCIPAL MOLINA over the P.A. system. The hallway fills with screaming and laughing STUDENTS on their way home. ESCALANTE's class stays at their desks. ARMANDO enters the classroom. ESCALANTE nods at him, and AR-MANDO proceeds to sweep the floor. The STUDENTS are used to the routine and lift their feet for him. For the most part, the KIDS in the hallway ignore MOLINA's speech. Those that do pay attention do so only to heckle or cheer at inappropriate times. Everyone else is glee-fully preparing to leave.)*

MOLINA'S VOICE *(overlapping above)*. Testing ... test-ing ... What? ... Oh, thank you ... *(Clears his throat.)* As you leave for vacation, I just wanted to wish everyone a Merry Christmas and a Happy New Year. I hope you all enjoy a happy and healthy holiday vacation ... Oh, also. If anyone has information regarding the missing typewrit-ers, I would greatly appreciate it. There will be no questions asked. Thank you... How do you turn this off? ... Oh, thank you. *(There is some static and the intercom cuts off. CLAUDIA and a few OTHERS look up from their work and longingly watch everyone leave. A group of STUDENTS walk by the class. Someone says, "Don't they ever leave?" The others laugh and joke as they walk off. ESCALANTE reads out loud from a test booklet.)*

ESCALANTE. Okay, see all those kids leaving school, climbing the hill to go home. Okay, that may be considered as a combination of two motions, horizontal and vertical. If the slope of the hill varies, the relation between the two rates of motion becomes complex. Got it? I doubt it. Who can explain this to me? Anybody? Come on, use the shortcut.

ANGEL. Kimo, this shortcut put me in the wrong neighborhood.

ESCALANTE. How 'bout you, Claudia?

CLAUDIA. Call on someone else, Kimo.

ESCALANTE. Come on, we're going backwards. This is ancient history. You can't forget what you learned last month. Come on, Claudia, think!

CLAUDIA. I don't feel like thinking.

ESCALANTE. You're foolin' around too much during the weekend. Girl's gotta do some work from the neck up. *(The STUDENTS laugh.)* We're gonna have to work straight through Christmas break. *(The STUDENTS groan.)*

CLAUDIA. Not me. *(She grabs her things and makes for an exit.)*

ESCALANTE. Where are you going? You late for another date? *(To class.)* Girl's got more boyfriends than Elizabeth Taylor.

CLAUDIA *(at the door).* I don't appreciate you using my personal life to entertain this class! *(She storms out. ESCALANTE signals for JAVIER to lead the lesson, then heads out after CLAUDIA.)*

ESCALANTE. Claudia ... *(Some STUDENTS rest their heads on their desks while OTHERS continue working. Maybe some take down the Christmas decorations. ESCALANTE runs over to CLAUDIA, who is crying in the hall.)* It's okay. It's okay. Talk to me ... Shhh. It's okay. *(He takes CLAUDIA by the arm and they walk farther away from the class.)*

CLAUDIA *(still crying).* Everything is falling apart right now. My boyfriend's freaking out, my mom. School sucks. I'm in that classroom all day, Kimo. Look at my clothes! And my hair. I can't even comb it! I hate my life.

ESCALANTE. At least you have hair to comb.

CLAUDIA. I hate math! I hate calculus!

ESCALANTE. No problem. I hate it, too. *(She laughs through her tears. ESCALANTE opens his arms and they hug. He smiles at her.)* Okay, get back in class before I get in trouble.

(CLAUDIA heads back to the classroom, wiping away the tears. MOLINA passes her as he crosses to ESCALANTE.)

MOLINA. Jaime, listen, I need a favor. Mr. Sanzaki resigned. He got his job back in aerospace. I need someone to cover his night school class.

ESCALANTE. No, no, Hugo, the test is a month away ...

MOLINA. Jaime, I'm in a jam. It's just until I replace him, okay?

ESCALANTE. I'm not going to be through with my calculus team till seven.

MOLINA. Great! The class starts at eight. Can you start tonight?

ESCALANTE. Eight o'clock? ... My family's never gonna forgive me. *(ESCALANTE starts for his class again. MOLINA calls after him.)*

MOLINA. Jaime, Think they'll pass the A.P. test?

ESCALANTE. Sure, sure. They're top kids.

MOLINA *(exiting)*. Got my fingers crossed. Keep up the good work. *(MOLINA strides off.)*

ESCALANTE *(to himself)*. Eight o'clock. Got a new class. Eight o'clock. *(ESCALANTE heads back to the class. Blackout.)*

SCENE THREE

AT RISE: *The Christmas decorations are gone. The STU-DENTS are all in their desks, looking more run-down than before. PANCHO is at the blackboard, working on a problem. ESCALANTE paces the room. He's agitated. He looks at PANCHO's attempt at an answer.*

ESCALANTE. Come on, Pancho. No way. This is easy. *(PANCHO tries again, stops, erases his work and begins again. He is getting frustrated and so is ESCALANTE.)* Put some energy into the upper quadrant of your stomach. Only got three weeks before the test. Use the short-cut! *(PANCHO stares intently at the problem. He takes another shot.)* No, no, no. C'mon! This is baby stuff, for Boy Scouts!

PANCHO. You know my mind don't work this way.

ESCALANTE. No excuses, Pancho. Tick-tack-toe. It's a piece of cake, upside down. Watch for the green light! *(PANCHO is exasperated. He stares at the board. Finally, he can't take it anymore and he punches the blackboard.)*

PANCHO. I been with you guys two years! Everybody knows I'm the dumbest! I just can't handle calculus, okay?! These guys have a better chance of making the A.P. test without me. *(JAVIER snickers.)* Don't laugh!

ESCALANTE. How can we laugh? You're breaking our hearts.

PANCHO. Don't do this, Kimo.

ESCALANTE. How noble. To sacrifice himself for the benefit of the team...Do you have the **ganas**? Do you have the desire?

PANCHO. Yes, I have the **ganas**!!

ESCALANTE. Do you want me to do it for you?!

PANCHO. Yes!!

ESCALANTE *(takes the chalk from him. To PANCHO).* You were supposed to say no. *(PANCHO goes to his seat. ESCALANTE draws a graph on the board as he talks to the class.)* I'm gonna have to get tough. Bullets are gonna have to start flyin'. Gonna have to stay late again. *(Everyone groans.)*

(ANGEL enters. He's out of breath as he takes his seat in the back.)

ANGEL *(whispering to TITO)*. What I miss?

ESCALANTE *(to ANGEL)*. The counselor was just here looking for you.

ANGEL. Hey, Kimo, it's cool, I was at the hospital...

ESCALANTE *(overlapping)*. Something about some cosmetology classes. He says there's three different levels. One for boys, one for girls, and one for, I don't know what kind. Why don't you go find out?

ANGEL *(overlapping)*. Oh, Kimo. Please listen, man. **Mi abuelita** fell down, hurt her hip, I had to get her taken care of—

ESCALANTE *(returns to the board. Overlapping)*. Check out. Game's over. You lose.

ANGEL. You never listen, man! You never listen to nobody!! **Te crees el más chingón!**

ESCALANTE. **Adiós.** Why don't you send me some postcards? Or call me on the telephone, let me know how you're doing. We love you.

ANGEL *(throws his desk over and grabs his crotch)*. Kimo Sabe this, **cabrón!** Huh?! *(ANGEL exits.)*

ESCALANTE. Hey, Pancho, I think that guy's got a bigger problem than you. *(He finishes drawing the graph.)* Tick. Tack. Toe. Simple. *(ESCALANTE looks around the room. No one is smiling. The lights fade into night.)*

(It is clearly after hours and the mood is subdued. The KIDS are sprawled all around the classroom, studying in pairs or small groups. They look ragged. ARMANDO is sitting on the hallway floor, working out a math problem. ESCALANTE is standing beside him. He seems tired and distracted.)

ESCALANTE *(re: ARMANDO's work)*. That's the wrong number, but you put it in the right place. You've got to watch the negative sign. Remember, it's a little stick that might trip you up. *(ARMANDO nods his head, crosses out a number, then puts in the right answer. He shows it to ESCALANTE.)*

ARMANDO. Like this?

ESCALANTE. That's it. You're the best.

ARMANDO. Thanks, Kimo. *(ESCALANTE wanders over to the class and peeks his head in the door.)*

ESCALANTE. All right. Synchronize watches, ready? Start the practice test: now. *(The KIDS mumble an acknowledgment and begin taking the practice test. ESCALANTE winces and massages his chest. He heads back over to ARMANDO.)*

ARMANDO. Working too hard, Mr. Escalante.

ESCALANTE. They'll be okay. They're tough kids.

ARMANDO. I was talking about you, Kimo.

ESCALANTE. No, come on, I'm the champ.

ARMANDO. You're working seven days a week. You should take a night off, take your wife and sons to the movies.

ESCALANTE. Twelve more days they got the test. Then, I go to junior high school to recruit for next year's class.

(ARMANDO returns to his work. ESCALANTE spots ANGEL, who has just entered the hallway. He's carrying some food.)

ANGEL. Heard there was some crazy **vatos** studying here late.

ESCALANTE. You're off the team. You blew it.

ANGEL. **Mi abuelita** thought they might be hungry. *(AN-GEL holds up the food as a peace offering. ESCALANTE turns away, but then catches a whiff of the food.)*

ESCALANTE *(interested)*. **Lomo montado? Pica a lo macho?** Where did your **abuelita** get the recipes for this?

ANGEL. I went to the library. Looked it up under Bolivian brain food. We're gonna need it.

ESCALANTE *(gives ANGEL a long, hard look)*. You gonna play by the rules?

ANGEL. I need calculus to get me a good job, Johnny...

ESCALANTE. You pull any tricks on me, I'll eat *you* for dinner... Get in there, you're way behind. *(ESCALANTE takes the food from ANGEL. ANGEL runs enthusiastically toward the classroom, then slams on the brakes, reverting back to his slow gang strut in front of the other kids. ESCALANTE sits beside ARMANDO. ARMANDO reaches for some food.)*

ARMANDO. Smells good. I hope they finish the test ahead of time.

ESCALANTE *(massaging his stomach)*. I've lost my appetite, lately.

(The lights fade into a tableau on the class. A solo spot comes up on JAVIER.)

JAVIER. Kimo reminds me a lot of my father... Not that they look alike, but that they're both so single-minded. My father started out picking grapes and nectarines in the San Joaquin valley—12 hours a day, six days a week. He taught himself at night by a kerosene lantern at migrant labor camps and succeeded in earning a G.E.D. by his 21st birthday. That's when he enrolled at Fresno

State and met my mother. Seven years to obtain his degree. Five days of harvesting to afford two days of higher education. On the day he graduated, he proposed to my mother, only he insisted on becoming a C.P.A. before raising a family. He made her wait four years before she finally heard her wedding bells. You have to admire a man with his patience and fortitude. But my father doesn't understand that what worked for him isn't necessarily gonna work for me. Back in his day, you could look down the road, see something in the distance, and be reasonably assured it would still be there when you arrived, no matter how long it took. But the world I live in isn't grapes and nectarines. It's two-way television, talking computers, genetic engineering—stuff that's gonna feel like ancient history by the time I graduate college. So I'm busy preparing myself for a future that's hard to see. I imagine worlds where cars skim through the air like boats on water. Sailing up to cities built a mile high, so that you can't tell the difference between clouds and windows. And everything self-cleaning, by design. Designs pioneered by Javier Perales... This my father calls daydreaming. My father's centrifugal force keeps me earthbound while I gaze upward to the heavens, through the prism of my own inner scope, imagining whole new worlds. In the time it takes to walk between social studies and gym class.

(The lights change back to daytime. The STUDENTS are still in their seats. They're exhausted. ESCALANTE is writing a problem on the board, pressing so hard that he breaks the chalk. He starts roving the aisles as he waits for the answer, his impatience mounting.)

ESCALANTE. We're looking for the area in the first quadrant bounded by the curve. What are the limits? Anybody?

CLAUDIA. Zero to pi over two, sir?

ESCALANTE. Wrong. Lupe?

LUPE. Uh, zero to pi over two?

ESCALANTE. What's wrong with you? This is review.

LUPE. Kimo, I checked my work twice.

ESCALANTE. I'm giving you the graph. Check it again.

TITO. No, Kimo. I got the same answer as the **gordita.**

LUPE. Don't call me **gordita, pendejo.**

ANA. It's zero to pi over two, sir.

JAVIER. Yeah, I got the same thing.

ESCALANTE. You guys should know this. No way! No way! You all took the shortcut, but you all took the *same wrong turn!* Green light means you *add.* Zero to pi over *four.* You should know this! What's wrong with you? This is review! You're acting like a blind man in a dark room looking for a black cat that isn't there! What's wrong with you guys?! I don't believe it! It's giving me a shot from the back! NO WAY! NO WAY!! *(ESCALANTE storms out. Silence.)*

PANCHO. Man, Kimo finally blew a head gasket. *(ESCALANTE enters the hallway, extremely upset. Suddenly, he grabs his arm and starts to massage it. He's in some pain. He stops short and massages his chest. He falls to his knees, clutching his chest. ESCALANTE collapses to the floor, gasping for air. He crawls a little way and then lies motionless, his breathing labored. RAFAELA has wandered out of the classroom to find ESCALANTE. She spies him on the floor.)*

RAFAELA. Ayúdenme...por el amor de Dios!! *(The OTHERS run from the classroom to see what the problem is. They find RAFAELA kneeling beside ESCA-LANTE. They gather around their fallen teacher.)*
LUPE. Somebody get a teacher!! *(PANCHO races off down the hallway. Blackout.)*

SCENE FOUR

AT RISE: *The STUDENTS hang out in the classroom. The team spirit is low. CLAUDIA is staring off into space. LUPE paces, PANCHO watches her. ANGEL is off by himself. TITO is quietly playing an instrument. RA-FAELA looks like she's been crying. ANA reads intently. JAVIER goes to ESCALANTE's desk and opens a book.*

JAVIER. Page 456, please...Come on, you guys. Four-fifty-six.
TITO. Will you shut up and sit down, man. *(Pause. JAVIER sits back down.)*
LUPE. He should have taken it easier.
RAFAELA. It's our fault. We just sit back and watch him burn in.
CLAUDIA. It's burn *out.*
PANCHO. He looked fine to me.
ANGEL. The man brought it on himself. He was asking for trouble.
ANA. How can you say that!?
PANCHO. What do you know? You're nothing but a wannabe **cholo** asshole, man.

ANGEL. At least I'm not pussy-whipped. *(PANCHO shoves ANGEL. They start fighting.)*

CLAUDIA *(overlapping)*. Stop it, guys!

ANGEL *(overlapping)*. You want me, Motorhead? Come on!

PANCHO *(overlapping)*. Come on, man, I'll kick your ass!

RAFAELA *(overlapping)*. Please, don't fight, please.

TITO *(unable to separate them, overlapping)*. Pancho! Cut the shit, man! Cool out! Just cool out!

(MOLINA enters.)

MOLINA *(overlapping)*. All right, all right! Break it up! Pancho! Just break it up. Now, settle down. *(The fight stalls. Everyone takes a deep breath and settles down. PANCHO shoots a dark look to ANGEL.)*

ANGEL *(to PANCHO)*. We'll talk later, ése.

MOLINA. All right, settle down, Angel, everybody, just sit down … Mr. Escalante is okay. He's recovering from a mild heart attack and he'll be under observation for the time being … I know there's only a couple of days before the A.P. calc exam, so Mrs. Ortega will be taking over the review. And I don't want to hear about any more trouble from this room … Angel, Pancho—I want you on your best behavior. You owe that much to Mr. Escalante. Now, can I trust you guys? … *(PANCHO and ANGEL nod.)* Okay. Get in your seats. *(The BOYS take their seats and MOLINA exits. The lights fade to a tableau. A spot comes up on TITO.)*

TITO. All I can hear is this white noise reverbing in my skull, ringing in my ears … Waves of sound that echo out of my body. Leaving me … Alone … Hollow … Empty … Except for one chord … One feeling. A whisper. Trying to get out. Making it hard to breathe ... One chord ... One song ...

(He picks up an instrument and starts to play a jarring, painful riff which slides into a soulful melody. When the music is done, the lights in the class return to normal. ORTEGA is at the front of the class. The STUDENTS are deadly silent.)

ORTEGA. Now, I know you're all a bit upset over Mr. Escalante's condition and so am I. Personally, I feel very badly about the whole thing ... I warned Mr. Molina something like this was bound to happen ... All we can do now is pray for a full recovery for Mr. Escalante ... And I hope the rest of us can learn from this experience ... Life is ultimately about balance. And compromise ... It's important to set goals, even ones that are difficult to attain. But finally, it's even more important to keep things in perspective. You have already accomplished far more than most high school seniors. In fact, if any student in this room were to decide not to take the A.P. test, no one could possibly hold it against you ... *(The STUDENTS eye each other. No one speaks.)* Unless anyone has any questions, why don't you all take the rest of this period off.

JAVIER. But the test is the day after tomorrow.

ORTEGA. I'm aware of that, Javier. But I think in this case, it couldn't hurt to take a little time away from calculus.

(ESCALANTE pokes his head into the room.)

ESCALANTE. *Hi!*

STUDENTS. Kimo! How are you?! Hey, Kimo Sabe! Kimo! *(They applaud as he enters.)*

ESCALANTE. I'm still alive! I'm a hard dyin' type of guy.

LUPE. Shouldn't you be in the hospital?

ESCALANTE. No, I should be here with you. Yeooowww! *(ESCALANTE crouches down and growls like a dog.)*

STUDENTS. *Bulldogs!!!!*

ESCALANTE. Thank you for baby-sitting my **canguros.**

ORTEGA. Well...It's seems as though I'm no longer needed here. Good to have you back, Mr. Escalante. *(ORTEGA exits.)*

ESCALANTE. Have a good day, Mrs. Ortega. *(The STUDENTS laugh. ESCALANTE roams the room like his old self.)* How are you? How are you?

TITO. Hey, you should be taking it easy, man.

ESCALANTE. Had to leave the hospital before they added up the bill.

ANGEL. Kimo, back to bed, homes.

ESCALANTE. No, I should be here with you guys. I mean, you already forgot to stand up! Come on! Come on! Stand and deliver. Everybody! Come on! *(The STUDENTS jump out of their chairs.)* No, no! Against the wall, like a snake! Hurry! *(The STUDENTS laugh and shout as they form a chain and snake around the room. The snake runs its course and stops with a line against the wall. ESCALANTE steps up to the front of the line. Overlapping above:)* Okay! We've been practicing for this all year. You're the best. You guys are the best! This is going to be a piece of cake!

STUDENTS *(in unison)*. Upside down!

ESCALANTE. And?

STUDENTS *(in unison)*. Step by step!

ESCALANTE. All right! You got it now. Get ready, keep your eyes open. *(To LUPE.)* Y equal to l n quantity x minus 1. What's the domain?

LUPE. X is greater than minus 1. *(ESCALANTE shoots LUPE. She goes to the end of the line.)*

ESCALANTE *(overlapping)*. No! I been gone one day and you forget already. Tito?

TITO. X is less than minus 1?

ESCALANTE *(gasping)*. No! End of the line! You're going to kill me, give me another heart attack. *(TITO goes to the end of the line. it's PANCHO's turn next.)* What's the domain?

PANCHO. All real numbers greater than 1. X is greater than 1.

ESCALANTE *(shakes PANCHO's hand)*. I told you you could do it! Okay, Kimo Sabe! You're the best!

PANCHO. All right! *(PANCHO proudly retains his place in line. ESCALANTE continues on. ANGEL is next. They stare at one another for a long moment.)*

ESCALANTE. Dog.

ANGEL. Dog.

ESCALANTE & ANGEL. Dog ... Dog ... Dog-dog-dog-dog ...

STUDENTS *(joining in)*. Dog-dog-dog-dog ... *(Lights down. The refrain continues through the blackout. End refrain.)*

SCENE FIVE

AT RISE: *Lights came up on the classroom. The desks have been straightened. The STUDENTS are seated, neatly spaced in rows. PRINCIPAL MOLINA is passing out test booklets.*

MOLINA. Anyone not here to take the Advanced Placement Test in calculus should now leave. All right, be sure that each mark is black and completely fills the answer space. If you make an error, you may save time by crossing it out rather than trying to erase it. It is not expected that everyone will be able to answer all the multiple choice questions... You may not use calculators, slide rules, or reference material. When you're told to begin, open your booklet, carefully tear out the green insert, and start to work... You may begin—now. *(The STUDENTS open the booklets and begin. They look intense, tired and under pressure. MOLINA prowls up and down the aisles. Perhaps there is a sound cue which helps indicate the excruciatingly slow passage of time... like a metronome. The STUDENTS work in total silence. We hear the occasional cough...A chair shifts... The lights fade to a tableau with a spot on TITO. He starts tapping his desk nervously. MOLINA stands near him. TITO stops... Two more lights come up, one on ANA, one on JAVIER. ANA fills in the correct answer and turns a page. JAVIER thinks for a moment, then writes in his test, trying to keep up with ANA...A light comes up on PANCHO. He's a little perplexed. He sighs, and erases an answer from his test booklet...A light comes up on RAFAELA. She is speaking softly to herself in Spanish. MOLINA crosses to her side, puts his finger to his lips and gently cautions her... Three more lights come up on ANGEL, CLAUDIA and LUPE. CLAUDIA has her head in her hands. LUPE is chewing her nails. ANGEL takes a deep breath, and plunges into the problem. Some of the KIDS are stuck, OTHERS start writing. MOLINA continues his vigil as the STUDENTS continue their painstaking work. After a while, the lights slowly fade out.)*

(The lights fade back up on MOLINA speaking. The classroom is full with STUDENTS, TEACHERS and FAMILY. There is a strong current of excitement throughout the room. Everyone is beaming.)

MOLINA. We, being teachers, know the Advanced Placement Tests are very difficult, especially in mathematics. Less than 2 percent of all high school seniors nationwide even attempt the A.P. test in calculus...I am proud to announce that no other school in Southern California has more students passing than Garfield High School. *(The GUESTS clap respectfully for the STUDENTS' achievement. ESCALANTE remains quietly proud. MR. DELGADO shakes his hand.)* Eighteen students took the test and 18 passed. Many with the highest score possible.

(ANGEL enters. He's drunk and wobbles as he walks, a big smile on his face. He bumps into a desk. Everyone notices him. ARMANDO nudges ESCALANTE.)

ARMANDO *(softly)*. Is he drunk?

ESCALANTE. No, he just walks like that. *(ANGEL joins his classmates. MOLINA tries to recover the moment.)*

MOLINA. It's because of the caliber of this graduating class that Garfield High is no longer under academic probation—Yes? *(RAFAELA has sidled up to MOLINA. She whispers in his ear. MOLINA steps aside and RAFAELA takes his place. TITO, CLAUDIA, ANGEL,*

LUPE, JAVIER, ANA, and PANCHO line up behind her. The GIRLS are holding ANGEL steady.)

RAFAELA *(slowly).* We have an announcement to make.

MOLINA. It's all right. *(Encouraging her.)*

RAFAELA *(smiling).* Okay. We, the A.P. calculus class, would like to present this plaque to our teacher, Jaime A. Escalante. *(ESCALANTE makes his way to the STUDENTS. They surround him as he reads the plaque. Embarrassed, ESCALANTE smiles and nods thankfully to the crowd. He tries to return to his place in the back. The KIDS don't let him leave.)*

RAFAELA. No, no. Read it out loud. Go ahead, don't be afraid.

ESCALANTE. "For improving our past, working tirelessly with the present, and shaping our future." *(ESCALANTE gets choked up. The STUDENTS laugh and give him a group hug, as everyone else applauds respectfully. Lights down.)*

SCENE SIX

AT RI^E: *The clapping continues through the blackout as the actors clear the stage. Lights come up on ANA, alone downstage, holding a letter.*

ANA. In most European nations, students attend classes six days a week. In Japan, they also attend classes at night. The average American student spends 2,000 more hours in front of the television than in school. Every six seconds a crime occurs on or near an American campus ... In one year, 338,000 students carried handguns into school at least once. More than 100,000 were armed every day ... Approximately one quarter of all major urban school districts are now using metal detectors and 74 percent of the students in those districts have witnessed either a killing, stabbing or shooting ... Nine of every 10 young people murdered in an industrialized nation are slain here in this country. In California, murder, theft, arson and robbery are committed more often by juveniles than by adults. And in many cities, homicide is now the leading cause of death among children. In half those cases, the killers are also children ... Gang participation has become the urban poor's version of teenage suicide ... According to the National Commission on Secondary Education for Hispanics, 40 percent of all Latino youths who drop out of U.S. schools, do so before the 10th grade ... Forty-five percent of Mexican American children never finish high school. When I started at Garfield High the dropout rate was 55 percent ... You can understand why graduation day was the most exciting day of my life ... Rafaela in her new dress ... Javier surprised me with a corsage. And papá invited the whole class to dinner at the restaurant. You should have seen how proud papá was of me when U.S.C. offered me a full academic scholarship. I calculated that it would cost more for my college diploma than my grandfather had earned in his entire life. As hard as it was, my straight A's were definitely worth the effort. I knew that I was not going to become just another statistic ... Three days after graduation, the letter came in the mail. (She begins to read from the letter.) "Dear Ms. Delgado ... I am writing to you because the Educational Testing Service

Board of Review believes there is reason to question your Advanced Placement calculus grades."

(Lights comes up on RAFAELA, TITO, LUPE and PAN-CHO. They too are holding letters.)

RAFAELA. What?

TITO. They gotta be kidding.

LUPE. Oh, please no, don't let it be true.

(Lights come up on CLAUDIA, ANGEL and JAVIER, also with letters. It is early summer, the STUDENTS have graduated. They should be happy, but they're not. Everyone is tense. The STUDENTS make their way into one group downstage.)

CLAUDIA *(reading)*. "Based on the unusual agreement of incorrect answers, the Educational Testing Service has no alternative but to question the scores of all the students with such unusual agreement."

PANCHO. English. What does it mean in English?

JAVIER. They're saying that we copied from each other, because we all had the same wrong answers.

LUPE *(sarcastically)*. We're too stupid to know how to cheat correctly.

ANA. Those letters don't go to our colleges, do they?

JAVIER. Of course they do. These are the guys who do the SAT'S.

ANA. But once they give you a scholarship, they can't take it back, can they?

ANGEL *(reading)*. "It's standard procedure to grade the test with the identity of the students concealed. Only after irregularities were found was it determined that the students who were in question were all from Garfield High School." *(CLAUDIA suddenly breaks down into tears. LUPE consoles her. Some of the KIDS head toward the classroom. JAVIER crosses over to ANA.)*

JAVIER *(softly)*. Anyone could have cheated. Pancho was way behind. Claudia freaking out all the time. Do you think someone got the test ahead of time?

ANA *(softly)*. No, but my father does.

(The lights crossfade as they make their way into the class and sit down. During the transition, ESCALANTE reads out loud from a letter.)

ESCALANTE *(reading)*. "This is a serious problem, and the E.T.S. would like to meet with you after you have read this letter and the enclosed pamphlet." You all received the same thing?

JAVIER. We can fight it. Take 'em to court. There's the Mexican American Legal Defense Fund and the A.C. L.U.

ANA. I'm supposed to start college in the fall.

RAFAELA *(quietly)*. We could retest. *(EVERYONE turns to her.)*

CLAUDIA. Taking the test again is like saying we cheated. It's an admission of guilt!

TITO. No way! I'm not gonna do it! I don't need to prove nothing to nobody.

ESCALANTE. These people are human. They could make mistakes, too.

JAVIER. Kimo, they're calling us cheaters! *(ESCALANTE looks at them one by one, looking for the truth in their eyes.)*

ESCALANTE. There was no need to cheat. You guys are the best. I'm gonna clear this up. *(ESCALANTE exits.)*

PANCHO. Shit, damn, shit! If I had taken that job with my uncle, I could have had a brand new car by now!

LUPE. Hey, it's okay. You're good with cars. You can fix yours.

CLAUDIA. Your girlfriend's accused of cheating and all you can talk about is your lousy car?

PANCHO. At least my car puts out! *(LUPE starts to cry. CLAUDIA comforts her.)*

CLAUDIA. You are such an *asshole*, Pancho!

(A deadly silence takes over the room. The group is broken up into factions—EVERYONE eyeing each other. No one talking. PRINCIPAL MOLINA, and DRS. PEARSON and RAMÍREZ enter the hallway. They cross toward the classroom.)

MOLINA. We would like to resolve this with as little publicity as possible.

PEARSON. Certainly, that is our intention as well.

MOLINA. I proctored the test. Everything was done according to your specifications. The desks were the required three feet apart. Here's a chart of where each student sat. *(MOLINA hands the chart to PEARSON.)*

RAMÍREZ. Mr. Molina, we understand this school has a history of break-ins.

MOLINA. That's true. But, no one ever broke into the safe. It's impossible. I assure you, only my secretary and I know the combination.

(ESCALANTE catches up with them.)

ESCALANTE. Hugo!

MOLINA. Jaime, this is Dr. Pearson and Dr. Ramírez of the Educational Testing Service. Gentlemen, Jaime Escalante. The A.P. calculus teacher.

PEARSON. Mr. Escalante.

RAMÍREZ. **¿Qué tal? Un placer.**

ESCALANTE. **El gusto es mío, señor.**

MOLINA. We were just on our way to the students.

ESCALANTE. Good. Let's go. *(ESCALANTE starts to lead them off.)*

PEARSON. I'm sorry, Mr. Escalante, but that's just not possible. E.T.S. policy.

ESCALANTE. But, they are my kids. I should be there.

RAMÍREZ. Mr. Escalante, this controversy is officially between the Educational Testing Service and the students. *(PEARSON, RAMÍREZ and MOLINA head to the classroom. ESCALANTE starts to follow them. MOLINA stops him. Exasperated, ESCALANTE relents. After a beat, he exits offstage.)*

(PEARSON, RAMÍREZ and MOLINA enter the classroom. The room gets very quiet.)

MOLINA. These gentlemen are from the Educational Testing Service. They've come a long way, so, let's cooperate with them as much as possible. *(More silence.)*

RAMÍREZ. Well...Does anyone have anything to say? *(Silence. MOLINA crosses to ANA.)*

MOLINA. Ana. I've known your family for years. Tell us the truth.

ANA. Nothing happened.

MOLINA *(bluffing)*. Now, don't lie to me.

ANA *(near tears)*. I'm telling you the truth! Nothing happened!

JAVIER. Why don't you just leave her alone? She didn't do anything wrong.

PEARSON. Then tell us who did. *(JAVIER gets out of his chair and walks out, slamming a door.)* We're not cops. We're not here to put anyone behind bars. If you cheated, let us know so you can go home and enjoy the rest of your summer. *(Silence. RAMÍREZ sits down next to RAFAELA.)*

RAMÍREZ. **Permiso**...I come from this neighborhood. **Yo vengo de este barrio.** And I know that sometimes we're tempted to take shortcuts. Just tell me the truth. What happened? Dime la verdad. *(RAFAELA looks around fearfully.)*

ANGEL. Okay. *(Pause. The STUDENTS look at him.)* We're busted. Why don't we just admit it?

RAMÍREZ. How'd you do it? *(Pause. ANGEL stands.)*

ANGEL. You sure no one gets in trouble, right?

PEARSON. As long as you tell us the truth. *(ANGEL looks around the classroom. EVERYONE waits expectantly.)*

ANGEL. I got the test ahead of time. I passed it around to everyone.

PEARSON *(pulls out a notebook, preparing to gather evidence)*. How did you get the test?

ANGEL. The mailman. I strangled him. His body's decomposing in my locker. *(The STUDENTS start laughing so hard they are practically on the floor. PANCHO crosses to ANGEL and gives him a high-five. TITO, ANGEL and PANCHO hug. The team is reunited. PEARSON and RAMÍREZ exchange a look.)*

RAMÍREZ *(to MOLINA)*. There's no sense in continuing if they won't cooperate. *(ANGEL thrusts his tattooed knuckles in RAMÍREZ' face. PEARSON and RAMÍREZ leave. MOLINA glares at the laughing STUDENTS.)*

MOLINA. If that's how you're going to behave, then just go home. *(The STUDENTS spill out of the classroom. Lights down.)*

SCENE SEVEN

AT RISE: *Lights come up on MOLINA and ESCALANTE in the classroom. ESCALANTE is pacing like a caged animal. MOLINA is holding a letter.*

MOLINA. Jaime, please, let me take care of this. It's an administrative problem. You're only the teacher.

ESCALANTE *(takes the letter from MOLINA)*. This I take care of myself.

(MRS. ORTEGA walks into the room.)

ORTEGA. You wanted to see me?

ESCALANTE. Do you know how this got in my box? *(Hands her the letter.)*

ORTEGA. What is it?

MOLINA. A letter of resignation ... Unsigned ... Anonymous.

ORTEGA. My guess is that it could have something to do with the scandal this school is facing.

ESCALANTE. Do you think they cheated? *(Pause.)*

ORTEGA. Mr. Escalante, you put those kids under an awful lot of pressure. They would have gone to any lengths to please you.

ESCALANTE. Do you think they cheated?

ORTEGA. I don't take any joy in your failure, Mr. Escalante. I recommended you for this job. On some level, I share the responsibility. The whole school does.

ESCALANTE. You didn't answer my question.

ORTEGA. All right. Well ... Every night when I go to bed, I watch the television news. I see a lot of people go on trial. They deny everything or their lawyers say they were insane when they did it. A lot of them get off ... But, I believe that most people who get caught today are guilty. Don't you, Mr. Molina? *(ORTEGA exits. ESCALANTE crumples up the letter.)*

ESCALANTE. Yep, it's true. Teaching dulls the senses ...

MOLINA. Jaime ... *(ESCALANTE doesn't say anything. MOLINA crosses to his side. They stand that way for a moment.)*

ESCALANTE. I may have made a mistake trying to teach them calculus.

MOLINA. Regardless of whether they passed that test or not, Jaime, they *learned.*

ESCALANTE. Yeah, they learned if you try real hard, nothing changes.

MOLINA. That's what you think? ... Then quit ... If that's all you have left to teach ... Quit.

ESCALANTE. You know what kills me, that they lost the confidence in the system that they're now finally qualified to be a part of...I don't know why I'm losing sleep over this. I don't need it. I could make twice the money, in less hours, and have people treat me with respect.

MOLINA. Respect? Jaime, those kids love you. They love you. *(They embrace. MOLINA exits.)*

(ESCALANTE slowly begins to organize his papers. A MARAVILLA GANG MEMBER drifts in. ESCALANTE eyes him. Neither of them speak. One by one the ENTIRE GANG makes their way in. The classroom is deadly silent. CHUCO and ANGEL enter and cross to ESCALANTE.)

CHUCO. **Orale**, Kimo Sabe...Kimo sabe **todo**. *(CHUCO holds out his hand. He and ESCALANTE shake hands, cholo-style.)*

ESCALANTE. **Orale.**

CHUCO. Homes told me you're havin' some problems. Just wanted to say, we got you covered.

ESCALANTE. Thank you very much.

CHUCO. We gonna cruise *downtown*, take action on those **pinche** E.T.S. boys. You gotta throw down, homes. Hit those **pendejos** where they live. Like you say, **ése**, teach them some manners.

ESCALANTE. I see...Tell you what. Let me try it my way first. That doesn't work, I'll let you know. Okay, Johnny?

CHUCO. Put the word out, bro. We'll back your play.

MARAVILLA GANG *(exiting)*. **Orale!** Kimo Sabe! **Orale! Orale!!**

ESCALANTE. **Orale.** Okay. (*The all head into the hall. ESCALANTE pulls ANGEL aside.*) Just tell me that wasn't your idea.

ANGEL (*conspiratorially*). It was Chuco's idea.

ESCALANTE. Goot. (*ESCALANTE pats ANGEL on the back. ANGEL follows the MARAVILLA GANG off.*)

(*PEARSON and RAMÍREZ have entered the classroom. They are looking over the "scene of the crime."*)

PEARSON. We're going nowhere here. I say we wash our hands of it.

RAMÍREZ. I think our best course of action is to turn the whole dispute over to the universities. Let the students appeal to whichever ones they've applied to.

(*They start to exit. ESCALANTE enters the classroom.*)

ESCALANTE. Good afternoon, Doctors...I feel I have the right to know why you think my students cheated.

PEARSON. Mr. Escalante, I appreciate your concern, but we're not at liberty to discuss the controversy with you.

ESCALANTE. Principal Molina proctored the test himself. His integrity has never been called into question and he has verified that nothing unusual took place. You investigated the test site personally. What have you found? Was anything out of order?

RAMÍREZ. It's an internal investigation for E.T.S. purposes only.

ESCALANTE. I would just like to see the test, that's all.

RAMÍREZ. Mr. Escalante, I understand what you're going through here, but, I repeat, the problem is between the

E.T.S. and your students. It doesn't reflect upon the school or its administration.

ESCALANTE. I would just like to see what kinds of mistakes were made. Once again, I'm their teacher. I know my kids.

PEARSON (to RAMÍREZ). If you're finished, we can leave. (PEARSON and RAMÍREZ move to exit. ESCALANTE cuts them off.)

ESCALANTE. Excuse me, but I'm not finished.

PEARSON. Mr. Escalante, as a mathematician, you're doubtlessly aware of the statistical improbability of having that many tests with identical wrong answers.

ESCALANTE. Maybe they all made the same mistakes because they all had the same teacher, teaching them the same program. I taught them step by step, inch by inch, all the way.

PEARSON. There were some...unorthodox, even illogical, computations for students of this caliber. Mistakes in simple math.

ESCALANTE. *I* may have made mistakes. They were way behind. We had to cram five years inside two. I had to teach them shortcuts.

PEARSON. Look, your students averaged fewer than four wrong on the multiple choice, while other schools average, what, 14 to 18 incorrect answers? And we found out that most of your kids finished the test with time to spare.

ESCALANTE. They should be rewarded, not punished.

RAMÍREZ. Mr. Escalante, the Educational Testing Service does not act capriciously. Every major university in the United States subscribes to our service.

ESCALANTE. I would just like to see the proof of wrong-doing. I would like to see the tests.

RAMÍREZ. Let me reiterate. There has been no proof of wrongdoing here. Only a suspicion of cheating.

ESCALANTE. In this country, one is innocent until proven guilty. Not the other way around.

RAMÍREZ. Just because we can't prove guilt doesn't mean we can sanction those scores.

PEARSON. If you're so confident of your students' abilities, why not encourage them to retest?

ESCALANTE. Why should I?

PEARSON. If they don't retest, everyone will assume they cheated.

ESCALANTE. Everyone will assume they cheated if they *do!* I want to see the tests, please!

RAMÍREZ. We're going around in circles here. Mr. Escalante, we're psychomatricians, thorough to the point of boredom. We're not out to get anyone here. *(PEARSON and RAMÍREZ try to exit, but again, ESCALANTE blocks the way.)*

ESCALANTE. Not so fast! If this was a simple situation of two students cheating, that's one thing. But, by making a blanket accusation, you're saying that there was a conspiracy. Every conspiracy has a leader! Who better qualified to be the leader than the teacher?!

RAMÍREZ. Mr. Escalante, nobody's accusing you of anything.

ESCALANTE. Not only me! The school, the parents, the entire community!

RAMÍREZ. Scores this high, I guarantee you, would be questioned regardless of the school.

ESCALANTE. Yes, but if this was Beverly Hills High School, they wouldn't have sent a black and a Latino to investigate.

RAMÍREZ. Mr. Escalante, I hope you're not insinuating that we haven't earned our positions here, 'cause no one's given me a damn thing...I suggest you're letting your emotions get the best of you.

ESCALANTE. If no one has given you a damn thing, you should not be taking away from my kids!

RAMÍREZ. The *identities* of the students were concealed until it was determined that irregularities existed.

ESCALANTE. Those scores would never have been questioned if my kids did not have Spanish surnames and come from **barrio** schools! You know that!

RAMÍREZ. All right. We've been patiently explaining our position and listening to your complaints. But *now*, our conversation is over.

ESCALANTE. There's something going on here that nobody is talking about! And you know what it is!

RAMÍREZ. No one has the right...to accuse me...of racism. *No* one has the right to *accuse me* of racism!

ESCALANTE. I know well how to spell discrimination! I thought this was over a long time ago. Why are you doing this to my kids?!

PEARSON. There are two kinds of racism, Mr. Escalante. Singling out a group because they're members of a minority and *not* singling out a group because they're members of a minority.

ESCALANTE. My kids could teach you a thing or two, Johnny!

PEARSON. All right. Enough is enough. It's high time we left.

ESCALANTE. Go for it! You didn't show me the tests. You didn't prove anything. My kids didn't do anything! I'm gonna prove you guys wrong! *(PEARSON and RAMÍREZ start to leave.)*

RAMÍREZ. This is not between you and us, Escalante.

ESCALANTE. Maybe not. But, if I catch you on the street, I'm gonna kick the shit out of you. *(PEARSON and RAMÍREZ exit. Lights down.)*

SCENE EIGHT

AT RISE: *Lights come up and a few of the STUDENTS are in the classroom. More are wandering in. ANGEL enters and walks to where TITO is sitting.*

ANGEL. My desk, man.

TITO. No, it was mine. *(ANGEL reaches underneath the desk and pulls something out from below. He rolls his fingers in front of TITO's face.)*

ANGEL. My boogers. My desk.

TITO. Your desk. *(TITO gladly moves. Most of the STUDENTS have gathered in the classroom.)*

(LUPE enters the hallway. PANCHO runs to catch up with her.)

PANCHO. Lupe, please, wait!

LUPE *(stops, but remains faced away from PANCHO)*. What do you want?

PANCHO. I need to talk.

LUPE. Now is not the time for this, Pancho. *(She starts to walk away. PANCHO musters his courage.)*

PANCHO *(slowly)*. I think about you every day...I can't get you out of my head...And...I'm afraid I'm never gonna see you again.

LUPE. You can't expect me to be your girlfriend at your convenience.

PANCHO. I'm an asshole. Sorry.

(PANCHO leans in to kiss her and LUPE melts into his embrace. CLAUDIA enters the hallway and sees the couple. She smiles as she passes by them and into the class.)

CLAUDIA. I thought I'd seen this place for the last time. *(PANCHO and LUPE break off the kiss and enter the classroom holding hands.)*

(ESCALANTE enters the hallway, heading for the class. The STUDENTS look up expectantly when he enters.)

PANCHO. Kimo, we graduated two months ago. What're we doing here?

ESCALANTE. Still somethin' I gotta teach you **burros**. Back in Bolivia, I was a professor in the top school. I emigrated to this country because I wanted my children to have a shot at the American dream. Not so easy. No one here understood me when I opened my mouth because "I mess up with the language." No matter how well I knew my subject, no matter how much I had to offer, there wasn't a single school which recognized my degrees from Bolivia. Everything I had accomplished back home added up to a big zero. Whole new ball game. Mopped the floors at Van De Kamps cafeteria. Bus tables in the day, learn English at night. I became cook in the restaurant. Two eggs and bacon, Bolivian-style. It would have been easy to give up. But I'll tell you what...I would not give in to their ignorance. Or to my own fears. I swallowed my pride. I enrolled at city college taking courses about subjects which I'd already taught. It was harder the second time, because now I had to support a family. I felt as if I was going backwards. And at times I was afraid I didn't have the **ganas** any-more. But I never thought I was beat. *Never*...Because I had a secret weapon...Knowledge...Knowledge is Power...It's something that can never be taken away from you...Like it or not, you're gonna be tested the rest of your lives. And the only time you fail is when you quit. When you let them take away your spirit...Your desire...Your **ganas.** *(The STUDENTS look at each other. Silence.)*

RAFAELA *(softly)*. I want to take the retest.

ANA. Me too. *(They look around to their classmates.)*

JAVIER. I won't do it. I won't retest. *(JAVIER gets up to leave.)*

ESCALANTE. We go as a team, or we don't go at all. *(JAVIER freezes at the door. ANA crosses to JAVIER, takes his hand and leads him back to his desk. Everyone looks to JAVIER.)* What do you say, Mr. Perales. In, or out? *(JAVIER looks at their expectant faces. He gives them the thumbs-up sign.)*

JAVIER. Count me in, Kimo. *(The STUDENTS wait nerv-ously as ESCALANTE heads out to the pay phone. He puts in a quarter and dials.)*

CLAUDIA. What's he doing?! What's he doing?! *(LUPE runs to the classroom door and relays the phone call to the KIDS.)*

LUPE. Shhh!!! He's on the phone!

ESCALANTE. Hello? This is Jaime Escalante ... My students have decided to take the test again ... You're kidding! ... Tomorrow? ...

LUPE *(relaying the info).* They say we gotta take it tomorrow! *(She looks fearfully to ESCALANTE.)*

VARIOUS STUDENTS *(overlapping).* No way! One day? How we gonna do it in one day?

LUPE *(to the class).* Shhh!!

ESCALANTE *(considers, then gives LUPE the thumbs-up sign).* Eight a.m., tomorrow. Thank you. *(He hangs up the phone. TITO, LUPE and CLAUDIA have spilled out into the hall.)*

TITO. No, Kimo. One day?

ESCALANTE. Can't do it in any less. I didn't make the rule. Gonna have to review the entire course in one shot. Okay, let's go! *(ESCALANTE ushers them back into the class.)*

CLAUDIA. Kimo, you're afraid we're gonna screw up royally tomorrow, aren't you?

ESCALANTE. Tomorrow's just another day, honey. I'm afraid you're gonna screw up the rest of your lives.

PANCHO. Maybe they'll give us the same test.

ESCALANTE *(gently).* Uh-uh. It'll be harder. You can count on that. Just go step by step and play defense. Don't bring anything. No pencils, no erasers, nothing. Don't wear clothes with too many pockets. Don't let your eyes wander. No spacing out. Don't give them any opportunity to call you cheaters. You are the true dreamers. And dreams accomplish wonderful things. You're the best. Tomorrow you'll prove that you're the champs. We're gonna start with Chapter 1... *(Lights slowly fade out.)*

SCENE NINE

AT RISE: *Lights up. PEARSON and RAMÍREZ are in the classroom along with several of the STUDENTS. PAN-CHO and LUPE are sitting near each other. RAMÍREZ places tests down on their desks. JAVIER enters along with a few others. As they enter, PEARSON gives each a pencil. Each student finds a desk.*

RAMÍREZ. Sit anywhere you like.

(The GROUP is almost complete. ANA enters.)

ANA. Excuse me? I'm going to have to leave early.

RAMÍREZ. What's wrong?

ANA. I have an appointment at U.S.C. It's related to my scholarship.

PEARSON. Can't it wait?

ANA. No, it can't. *(PEARSON and RAMÍREZ exchange a look.)*

RAMÍREZ. Okay. Just do as much as you can.

(ANGEL arrives barechested, wearing only shorts with the pockets turned inside out. He throws his hands over his head like a prisoner being searched. PEARSON shakes his head and hands him a pencil. ANGEL accepts the pencil and flashes his knuckles at PEARSON.)

PEARSON. Please take a seat. *(ANGEL sits. PEARSON closes the doors. RAMÍREZ directs ANA to a seat near the door and counts the STUDENTS.)* I'm sure you are all familiar with the procedure. You have 90 minutes to complete the multiple choice section. Do not fill in answers by guessing. Wrong answers will be counted against you. Credit will be given for partial solutions. Do not spend too much time on any particular answer. You may open the booklet, and, begin. *(The STUDENTS do so. This test is far more daunting than the first test. RAMÍREZ and PEARSON constantly prowl up and down the aisles.)*

(A light comes up on ESCALANTE. He's alone, pacing nervously, talking to himself, willing the STUDENTS to do their best.)

ESCALANTE. It's okay ... You're the best ... Just go step by step ... Play defense ... *(As if in response to ESCALANTE, the STUDENTS begin to tackle the problems. During the following dialogue RAMÍREZ and PEARSON should never acknowledge that any of the STUDENTS are speaking out loud.)*

JAVIER *(slowly)*. One. A particle moves along the x-axis so that its acceleration at any time t is given by a(t) equals 6t minus 18 ...

CLAUDIA *(softly)*. I hate math ... I hate calculus ...

ESCALANTE. No problem, I hate it too ... Stay calm.

ANA *(softly)*. Not enough time, not enough time ...

ESCALANTE. You can do it ...

JAVIER & CLAUDIA. At time t equals 0 the velocity of the particle is v(0) equals 24, and at time t equals 1 its position is x(1) equals 24 ...

TITO. White noise, ringing in my ears ...

ESCALANTE. You're the champs.

RAFAELA. I tried so hard, Mama, I really did ...

ESCALANTE. You can do it ...

TITO. Waves of sound ... Empty ... Alone ...

JAVIER, CLAUDIA, ANA & ANGEL. (a) Write an expression for the velocity v(t) of the particle at any time t ...

PANCHO. You know my mind don't work this way! Everybody knows I'm the dumbest! I just can't handle calculus, okay?!

ESCALANTE *(gently)*. Come on, Pancho. Tick-tack-toe. Piece of cake.

CLAUDIA, ANA, ANGEL, TITO & RAFAELA. (b) For what values of t is the particle at rest?

LUPE. **Diosito Mio, por favor,** I'm just so tired ...

ESCALANTE *(teasing)*. Hey, Señorita, no spacing out, tomorrow you sleep.

CLAUDIA, ANA, ANGEL, RAFAELA & TITO *(overlapping)*. (c) Write an expression for the position x(t) of the particle at any time t.

ESCALANTE *(overlapping)*. Watch for the stick, it'll trip you up ...

JAVIER *(overlapping)*. I can see worlds where cars skim through the air like boats on water ...

ESCALANTE *(overlapping)*. Knowledge is power. Your Secret Weapon ...

CLAUDIA *(overlapping)*. Someplace to relax, someplace to breathe, pushing, pushing ...

ANGEL, TITO, RAFAELA, JAVIER, LUPE & PANCHO *(overlapping)*. (d) Find the total distance traveled by the particle from t equals 1 to t equals 3.

ANA *(overlapping)*. Dear Ms. Delgado, the E.T.S. believes there's reason to question your A.P. test grades...

ANGEL *(overlapping)*. Not around here, homes. Not in East L.A. ...

LUPE, PANCHO, RAFAELA, TITO & CLAUDIA *(overlapping)*. The Board doubts that the grades are valid due to these unusual circumstances...

ESCALANTE *(overlapping)*. You don't ever give up! You don't ever give in!

ALL STUDENTS *(overlapping)*. It's standard procedure to grade the test with the identity of the students concealed...

ANGEL. Fear is my friend.

ALL STUDENTS. Step by step, inch by inch, no free rides.

ESCALANTE. You are the true dreamers, and dreams can accomplish wonderful things...

ESCALANTE & STUDENTS. Step by step, inch by inch, no free rides. *(The chant continues as the lights fade out.)*

SCENE TEN

AT RISE: *Lights up. The KIDS are scattered around the class, anxiously awaiting the results. PRINCIPAL MOLINA and ESCALANTE are in the hallway. ESCALANTE is pacing.*

MOLINA. They probably got stuck in traffic.

ESCALANTE. I didn't get stuck.

MOLINA. Do you want to send the kids home?

ESCALANTE. No. We wait. *(Checks his watch.)*

MOLINA. Oh! Did I tell you? There's good news. The computers arrived!

ESCALANTE. Yep. That'll do it.

(He and MOLINA continue waiting. Finally, PEARSON and RAMÍREZ stride down the hall. They stop in front of the classroom.)

ESCALANTE. Do you have a late pass? No? Too bad. *(The E.T.S. MEN share uncomfortable smiles. The FOUR head into the class. A few KIDS discreetly whisper, "Late. Late." Someone calls out, "Give 'em the chair." RAMÍREZ opens his valise and takes out the results. The room gets deadly silent.)*

RAMÍREZ. As you know, A.P. tests are graded on a scale from one to five. A grade of one or two is failing. Three or four is passing. Five is a perfect score. *(Pause.)* Delgado, Ana: 4. *(ANA and JAVIER hug. RAFAELA stands when her name is called.)* Fuentes, Rafaela: 4. *(The class lets out a small cheer. RAMÍREZ has to speak up. A bit louder.)* Escobar, Guadalupe: 4. *(LUPE jumps up and screams. CLAUDIA and she jump up and down in each other's arms. The excitement builds. RAMÍREZ continues, louder.)* Guitano, Tito: 4. *(TITO shouts and does a drum roll on his desk. Louder.)* Perales, Javier: 5. *(The class roars its approval ESCALANTE goes over to JAVIER and shakes his hand.)*

PEARSON. Quiet! Please! Just a few more. *(The class settles down a bit.)*

RAMÍREZ. Camejo, Claudia: 4. *(CLAUDIA rejoices.)* Garcia, Francisco: 3. *(PANCHO jumps up and shouts. He and LUPE kiss.)* Guerra, Angel: 5. *(The STUDENTS cheer. The celebration gets out of control. RAMÍREZ hands the results to MOLINA. MOLINA shakes hands with PEARSON and RAMÍREZ. The THREE of them exit.)*

ANGEL. Kimo, Kimo, Kimo, Kimo... *(The STUDENTS join the chant and pick up ESCALANTE onto their shoulders.)*

STUDENTS. Kimo, Kimo, Kimo, Kimo, Kimo... *(The chant fades out as each STUDENT steps forward to deliver the tally for Garfield High's calculus program.)*

LUPE. In 1982 Garfield High School had 18 students pass the A.P. calculus exam.

PANCHO. In 1983 Garfield High School had 31 students pass the A.P. calculus exam.

RAFAELA. In 1984, 63 students.

TITO. 1985, 77 students.

CLAUDIA. 1986, 78 students.

JAVIER. In 1987 Garfield High School had 87 students pass the A.P. calculus exam.

ANA. When I started at Garfield it was in danger of losing its accreditation. By 1988 it had produced more Advanced Placement calculus students than all but three public schools in the entire nation.

ANGEL. If the average spray can covers 22 square feet and the average letter is three square feet, how many letters can a tagger spray with 3 cans of paint?

ESCALANTE *(overlapping)*. Okay, that's it, the chair for you, Johnny.

ANGEL. Just kidding, just kidding. *(Lights out.)*

END OF PLAY

ADDITIONAL CHARACTER NOTES

- JAIME ESCALANTE: Wears glasses and a white motorman's cap.

- JAVIER PERALES: Wears glasses. College prep all the way.

- TITO GUITANO: Handsome, ultra-cool. A dreamer.

- CLAUDIA CAMEJO: Tries to reject traditional Mexican-American values.

- FRANCISCO "PANCHO" GARCIA: Overweight. Has low expectations of himself. A bit reckless.

- LUPE ESCOBAR: Extremely social, gossipy, popular, trustworthy, overweight.

- ANA DELGADO: Demure, diffident, shy, brilliant. Inner strength.

- RAFAELA FUENTES: Has trouble with English. Dislikes drawing attention to herself.

- ANGEL GUERRA: Volatile, tough, philosophical, clever with a wise-guy sense of humor. Confronts life head-on.

- ARMANDO: Has high aspirations.

- HÉCTOR DELGADO: Proud, strong-willed.

GLOSSARY

abogado - lawyer
animales salvajes - wild animals
Ayúdenme ... por el amor de Dios! - Help me ... for the love of God!
balas - bullets
bienvenido - welcome
canguros - kangaroos
carnal -blood brother
carnitas de puerco - shredded pork
cholos - gang members
como en tu casa - same as in your house
Con todo mi amor y que Dios te bendiga. - With all my love
   and may God bless you.
Desaparecidos - The ones who disappeared
Dime la verdad. - Tell me the truth.
El Ciclón - The cyclone
El gusto es mío, senor. - The pleasure is mine, sir.
el pecho - the chest
Entienden inglés? - Do you understand English?
ése - dude
Espera afuera. - Wait outside
gabachos - white boys
ganas - desire
gordita - fatty
helado de chocolate - chocolate ice cream
Lomo montado - special Bolivian dish
Los que no entienden inglés, por favor levanten la mano. -
   Those who don't understand English, please raise your hand.
Los que no hablan inglés, por favor, pasen al frente. -
   Those who don't speak English, please come to the front of
   the room.
mi abuelo - my grandfather
Mi misma sangre - my same blood

mi pueblo - my hometown

mocoso - snot nose

Mucho gusto - Pleased to meet you

No sé - I don't know

Nuestra senora la Reina de los Angeles. - Our Lady Queen of Los Angeles.

Orale! - All right!

Oye como va - Listen how it goes

pelón - baldy

pendejo - pubic hair

Pica a lo macho - special Bolivian dish

pinche - goddamn

Ponte trucha - Get with it

Pues ni modo - No way

puto - male whore

Qué dijo - What did he say?

quetzales - Guatemalan currency

Quiché - a Mayan language

Qué tal? Un placer. - How are you? A pleasure.

Qué te pasa? - What's wrong?

ruca - girl

Sabe qué, ése? - You know what, dude?

**sangre por sangre, carne de mi carne, vida por vida...
Barrio** - blood for blood, flesh of my flesh, life for life... the 'hood

sufriendo - suffering

Te crees el mas chingón! - You think you're the biggest stud!

tírame un beso - throw me a kiss

todo - everything

un soldado - a soldier

vatos - dudes

vivo - alive

Yo soy el padre de la niña, no usted! - I'm the girls's father, not you!